Reminiscences of a Nearly Somebody

Peter Morrell

ISBN: 978-1-8380929-5-5

Best wishes ~

Also by Peter Morrell

Fiction
The Rector of Pepynbridge
The Islamist of Pepynbridge
The Honourable Member for Pepynbridge

Non-Fiction
The Russells of Thornhaugh
From the Pulpit, Home and Abroad

Reminiscences
of a
Nearly Somebody

Five Essays

Peter Morrell

Published by i2i Publishing. Manchester.
www.i2ipublishing.co.uk

To
Wendy
who persuaded me to pen
Wandervogel

and to
Peter
who, after reading Wandervogel in draft,
encouraged me to publish it

and to
Mary
my ever patient
and supportive
wife

Collared

***

Wandervogel

Introduction

The account that follows is of a walk I took alone, aged 18, through the Rhineland and the Black Forest in April and May 1963, as I finish this in March 2021, nearly 58 years ago.

I kept no diary of my walk and, inevitably, the passage of time has erased from my memory the names of those I met and with whom I talked. With the exception of a group of teenagers who shared a dormitory with me in a youth hostel in Heidelberg one night, and Joshua, an American aged about 20 who I encountered in Freiburg, all encounters were with Germans much older than I and, as less than 18 years had elapsed since the end of the war in Europe, the occasionally startling content of some of the conversations I had with them has remained with me. The reader may wonder about the accuracy of my recollection of those conversations. As I recount in **Hustings**, I have been a political animal since the Suez debacle in 1956. The Germans with whom I spoke betrayed political sentiments formed in the cauldron of the Second World War that made a profound impression upon me at the time and remain as vivid today as they were when I heard them. Whilst I may not have reproduced the precise phraseology employed, in every case the substance is accurate and it is why I decided to share this account with you, the reader.

Although places are, with one exception, correctly named, I have given some people I met in Germany pseudonyms. In the event of any of them reading this, I hope they will forgive me and, if they remind me of their true name, I shall correct it in the next edition, if there is one.

During my time in Germany, I only spoke English during the two days I spent in the company of Joshua. All other conversations were conducted in German. However, in the narrative that follows, I have recounted them in English, while occasionally inserting a German phrase or title.

As I explain more fully in **The Beginning**, I decided upon the walk in order to improve my spoken German. However, the title, **Wandervogel**, which translates as 'Bird of Passage', reflects the unintended consequence that, as well as the walk being a passage through a fair portion of what was then West Germany (the Federal Republic of Germany, or FRG), it became a passage to adulthood.

*

with wrought iron tables and chairs, shrugged off my rucksack, placed it on the ground and sat down.

A waiter approached and, to his credit, displayed none of the disdain he may well have been feeling at seeing such a modestly clad and scruffy customer.

"Yes, Sir?"

"I'd like a beer, please," I said. Then, a smidgeon of caution entered my consciousness.

"How much will it cost?"

The waiter quoted the equivalent of one pound sterling in deutschmarks and registered the consternation that then crossed my features. As his next words disclosed, he was a kind man at heart, who approved of this solitary *Wandervogel*, who had chosen to tramp all the way up the hill on such a hot morning in the hope of liquid refreshment.

"It is a lot of money," he observed.

"It is," I replied, "and I cannot afford it."

He smiled and then,

"I don't expect you can, my friend. What a pity." I nodded. He added, by way of explanation, "You know, this inn is quite famous."

"Is it?"

"Yes, it is. Your Duke of Edinburgh sometimes stays here."

Together, we laughed gently and I took my leave, wandering rather more comfortably back down the hill to the river and the next village, where I stopped for a beer and an early lunch. I limited myself to one beer and walked on to Heilbronn, where I intended to stay the night, arriving in the late afternoon.

*

My recollection today of the city I visited in mid-April 1963 is that much of it presented as modern. Blocks of flats and offices dominated. I do not recall any old buildings specifically, although, glancing at websites when writing this, there are some. My subsequent research has disclosed that Heilbronn was very heavily bombed by the Allies during World War II. Raids began in 1940, when minor damage was caused, but, on 10 September 1944, the city was carpet bombed. One thousand, one hundred and sixty-eight bombs fell, killing 281 residents.[4]

I made my way towards the centre of the city, intending to find an inn for the night, but lacked information about what was available and where a suitable one might be found. On a large, open-air, paved terrace, overlooking the centre of the city, I spotted a slim woman carrying a shopping bag, who, I guessed, was in her thirties. I approached her. I explained what I was doing, and that I was looking for a modest inn to spend the night.

"You're English, aren't you?" Her tone was not unfriendly.

"Yes, I am."

She looked intently at me, sizing me up.

"Well, there's an inn up there..." she gestured to her right, "... about a kilometre away, but I advise you not to go there."

"Why not?"

"They're all Nazis in there. They don't like the English. They'll not treat you kindly."

She gave me directions to another hostelry which she judged would be suitable, which it was, as I later discovered. However, that was not quite the end of our conversation. Whether she asked me if I knew someone in Manchester, or wherever, and whether we discussed the dreadful winter that had just passed, I cannot remember now, but what I do recall her saying was,

"Tell me, why did you bomb Heilbronn? Before the war, it was a beautiful city, but look at it now."

She waved towards the modern blocks.

"Before the war ..." I started.

"Yes?"

"Was there any industry in Heilbronn?"

"There certainly was."

"And, what was it?"

"We used to make precision instruments. We were well known for it."

Innocently, I thought, she had disclosed a very good reason why the Allies had bombed Heilbronn, but I decided not to be drawn.

"What a shame," I said.

She nodded. I continued,

"I'm afraid I can't say why we bombed Heilbronn. I simply do not know." Which was true. I didn't know for sure, even though I could guess.

We parted on friendly terms and I sought out the inn she had recommended. I ate dinner and spent the night there and have no recollection of meeting any self-proclaimed Nazis or hearing any anti-English sentiments expressed whilst I was there. The woman had done me a favour, for which I was grateful.

*

The following morning, I walked to Maulbronn, where I knew there was a monastery, but my guidebook had left me totally unprepared for the magnificence and beauty of what I encountered.

There are number of websites describing the monastery buildings and their surroundings and I encourage the reader to Google 'Maulbronn Monastery'[5] and click on 'Images' where there are displayed many views of the beautiful buildings and their surrounds.

Maulbronn Monastery, Baden-Württemberg, Germany
Photo © Image by PixelDino from Pixabay

The website informs that, from 1147, when construction began, it was a Cistercian monastery. The oldest parts of the complex are Romanesque, but *"it was there that Gothic design was first implemented in the German-speaking world."*[5] The abbey church is majestic and the cloisters, preserved in their original completeness, provide a haven of beauty, peace and tranquillity. The monastery functioned until the Reformation, when, its website informs the reader,

> Duke Christoph of Württemberg, converted the complex into a Protestant boarding school. Its pupils included prominent scientists and writers including Johannes Kepler, Friedrich Hölderlin and Hermann Hesse. The school still exists, but is called today Evangelical theological seminary.[5]

Thirty years after my visit, Maulbronn Monastery was deservedly named a UNESCO World Heritage site.

I was entranced by the whole experience, made all the sweeter by catching me totally unawares and my memory today, admittedly refreshed by the images on the monastery's website, is still bright. I spent happy hours there, wandering through the ecclesiastical buildings, tarrying in the cloisters and exploring other buildings within the complex.

*

The next morning, I was on the road again, this time to the city of Pforzheim, where I dined in a modest restaurant and overnighted in a youth hostel. Pforzheim sits at the northern edge of the Black Forest and is remarkedly similar to Heilbronn. Research reveals them to be about the same size, each with some 120,000 inhabitants. Before World War II, like Heilbronn, Pforzheim hosted factories that manufactured precision instruments. It was also believed by the Allies to be a transport centre for the movement of troops and so, not unreasonably, it was a target for massive Allied bombing.[6] Looking at a website, as in 1963, today modern buildings predominate. I recall having no significant conversation there and so, as I did then, I move on to Baden-Baden, 37½ miles distant by road. I must have overnighted on the way, where I cannot say, but was thrilled when I reached this most beautiful city.

*

Noted for its natural springs, Baden-Baden has been a spa town since Roman times. It lies in a valley on the edge of the Black Forest and is treasured for its stunning *Kurhaus* (Spa Resort) (overleaf), constructed between 1821 and 1824, distinguished by its unique *Belle Époch* style elegance. Nearby is the *Trinkhalle* (Pump House) (also overleaf), another architectural gem.

   In the nineteenth century, Baden-Baden was a much-loved gathering place for the rich and famous of Europe, including, amongst others, Queen Victoria. Its elegance and tranquillity

Kurhaus, Baden-Baden, Baden-Württemberg, Germany
Photo © Image by Stefanie Laubscher from Pixabay

Trinkhalle, Baden-Baden, Baden-Württemberg, Germany
Photo © Image by edysign from Pixabay

made it a pleasant place to wander about, which I did, before finding my way to the general post office, where I collected another letter from my mother. As I had done previously, I

responded with a postcard, displaying one of the lovely buildings that I had seen earlier that day. I rested in Baden-Baden for
a full day and two nights, before setting out eastwards towards
the Black Forest.

*

for a long time. Then they caught a whiff of my scent and, as one, raised their heads, glanced in my direction, turned and pronked into the forest on the farther side of the stream. Since that day, I have watched hundreds of deer, both in Northamptonshire and Scotland, but that was the first occasion I had ever seen them outside a zoo.

*

Whenever I stopped in a pub for lunch or booked into an inn or youth hostel for the night, I invariably met and conversed with people, all of them German, with the exception of the American I mention in the **Introduction** and whom we shall meet shortly. In April and May in Germany, as in England, it was term-time and children and young people were in school, so, apart from the teenagers I met in the youth hostel in Heidelberg, fresh from their visit to the Verdun battleground, everyone I encountered and talked with was an adult. Again, as I have already mentioned, conversations nearly always began with questions about where I came from, whether I knew so-and-so who lived somewhere in England and how awful the previous winter had been. Sometimes, it ended there, but other times it did not.

On one occasion, I met and chatted with a man aged thirty-nine or forty, as it turned out. Our conversation progressed to the Second World War, which it often, but not always, did.

He said,

"I was in Scotland once."

"Oh," I replied, "were you?"

"Yes."

"Where?"

"I cannot remember, but it was in the far north somewhere. It was very cold and very wet and in the winters it snowed a lot."

I noted his use of the plural.

"How long were you there?"

"Two years."

"And why were you there?"

"I was a prisoner of war."

I digested this and wondered how to progress our chat. I needn't have worried. He had something he thought important to impart to this Englishman, too young to have known the war. He was right.

"In 1942, I was sent to the Eastern Front. I was only eighteen."

"My age," I remarked.

"Yes, your age."

"What was it like?"

"Terrible!" He paused. "It was Hell. Thousands of soldiers being killed. Awful! I hate remembering it now. I was so glad when they brought me back."

"Oh, when was that?"

"1944. I was sent to France. To the Western Front after you had invaded."

"What was that like?"

"Well, not so bad as the Eastern Front, but it wasn't good. By then, we knew we were beaten."

He paused again, pondering what to say next. I kept silent. Then he continued,

"One day, I was walking on my own along a lane in a wood in Northern France."

"Were you armed?"

"Of course. I had my rifle hanging on my shoulder. And the lane turned a corner and, when I walked round it, you know what happened next?"

"No. What?"

"There were some American soldiers walking towards me. I put my hands up and said '*Gott sei dank* (God be thanked)!' They took me prisoner. I was so happy. I was taken to a camp in France and, after that, to the camp in Scotland."

He frowned and shook his head vigorously.

"War is terrible! We must never do it again. Remember that, my young English friend. No more war! Never!"

"I agree."

"Good! *Auf wiedersehen* (Goodbye)."

"*Auf wiedersehen.*"

And that was the end of it. I forgot to thank him for telling me what he had done, but I was glad he had, as the fact that it remains fresh in my mind to this day testifies.

*

One afternoon, the solemnity and spell of the forest, filled as ever with the bewitching calls of cuckoos, was disturbed by a distant but persistent buzzing. It sounded too mechanical, I concluded regretfully, to be naturally generated. I frowned and looked at my map. A mile or so in front of me, there was, I saw, a tortuously curling road, not unusual in the increasingly precipitous landscape I was encountering as I progressed southwards and eastwards. What was unusual, I concluded, as I drew closer and the noise grew louder, was that the noise was continuous and clearly the product of more than one vehicle. Many more than one, I discovered, as I breasted a ridge and saw the road ascending the steep slope below me. I had happened upon a hill-climb competition. I sat amidst the trees, some three hundred yards or so above what was clearly the end of the course, marked with flags and manned by stewards. Most of the rest of it coiled up the slope within my line of sight.

I must have sat there for over an hour and watched as sports cars, mainly hard-top Porsche 356 Bs and open Jaguar E-Types, howled and wound their way upwards. The Porsche 356 B had been introduced into the Porsche range in 1960 and was manufactured until it was replaced in 1964 by, amongst other models, the soon-to-be famous 911. The Jaguar E-Type was first marketed in March 1960 and I remember well the day, later that same year, when, with school friends, I admired parked in Dean's Yard, Westminster, the first one I had ever seen. I still think the open Jaguar E-Type is the most beautiful sports car ever manufactured, but, on that afternoon in the Black Forest, it was no match for the Porsches. The bends were sharp and the rear-engined Porsches rounded them as if glued to the tarmac, while, driven at competitive speed, the front-engined E-Types lost their rear ends at almost every corner. Victory went to the Porsches, which, I thought then, were neither as elegant, nor as beautiful, as the sleek growler from Coventry.

Jaguar E-Type
Photo © Image by 8832037 from Pixabay

I did not tarry until the end. There came a moment when I glanced at my wristwatch and realised that, if I were to reach the village where I had planned to stay before nightfall, I needed to be on my way.

Another imposing building in Freiburg is the Merchant Hall (*Historisches Kaufhaus*), built between 1520 and 1530 in the same Gothic style and red sandstone as the Münster.

Historisches Kaufhaus Freiburg, Baden-Württemberg, Germany
Photo © Image by Couleur from Pixabay

Freiburg still boasts two medieval gates, one of which, the Martin Gate (*Martinstor*), is particularly fine. It was extensively remodelled in 1905, but retains much of its earlier grandeur. And it would be remiss not to mention that Freiburg hosts the Albert Ludwig University, the fifth oldest in Germany.

*

That evening in the youth hostel, we discussed what we had seen in Freiburg and other topics of mutual interest, which would have certainly included John Kennedy, elected President of the United States of America in 1960 and, in the spring of 1963, an iconic figure for young people the world over. Then

Joshua suggested that next day we should visit Hohengerold-seck Castle.

"Why?" I asked.

"Oh, I went there on my way here. It's great and I'd like to show it to you."

"Well, thanks, but how far is it?"

"Oh, about fifty miles. Not far by car."

I agreed and I am glad I did.

We arrived at about eleven o'clock. Joshua parked the car and we walked from the car park to the ruined castle, which took some forty-five minutes.

The castle was built in the mid-thirteenth century on top of a hill and was destroyed in 1688. However, much of its structure remains and Joshua and I climbed onto the roof of the upper castle and gazed out over a stunning landscape.

*

Before I continue, another digression. I have already mentioned Hugo Garten, who taught German to the A-Level French and German pupils at Westminster School. Ernst Sanger, who hailed originally from Vienna, also taught us German and took members of the Modern Languages set, including me, on educational summer holidays; in 1961, to Mayrhofen in the Austrian Tyrol; and in 1962, to Santander in Northern Spain. The Modern Languages A-Level set was taught French by Geoffrey Shepherd. His initials were G.A.S. and, out of his hearing, GAS was what we called him, although he probably knew that. GAS was an interesting man, who not only taught us French, but, from to time, branched out to discuss French and German political history. His father was English, but his mother was German, and GAS spoke her language fluently. He had served in the British Army as a tank commander during World War II. After the defeat of Germany, British Intelligence persuaded him to remain in Germany to re-educate former members of the Hitler Youth (*Hitlerjugend*). As he explained one day, one of the psychological bulwarks employed to significant effect by the Nazi Party was the mystical association between the landscape of Germany and the German *Volk* or people. Forests represented hidden power and mystery. Rivers equated to the latent strength of the Aryan race. Their invincible power had carved valleys out of rocky terrain, thrusting through it, casting impeding rock aside and, like the *Volk*, forcing a way through the toughest of opposition. It was a theme that was often evoked in nineteenth century German literature and reflected in Wagner's music and operas; and it formed an important component of the message proclaimed by the Nazi Party. The Nazis frequently held torch-lit processions, manned by uniformed Party members and symbolic of rivers, that paraded through towns and cities, emblematic of the Party's insistence that nothing could prevail against a united Aryan *Volk*; a *Volk* committed to casting opposition aside, enabling its will to prevail against all odds and its ideology to vanquish inferior cultures.

It was from that pernicious psychological delusion that Geoffrey Shepherd set out to disabuse the young German Nazis committed to his care.

"I failed," he told us. "One day, in the Rhineland, as we often did, we went for a walk in the countryside and, at the suggestion of one of my charges, we climbed up onto the battlements of a castle. Before us lay an archetypical German landscape of forest-clad hills, shrouded here and there by coils of mist and cleft by deep valleys. It was the image that I had been spending my time trying to convince my young charges was just a landscape and betokened nothing more. As we gazed in silence, a young German, aged I suppose about eighteen, put one arm around my shoulders and, raising the other, he pointed to the view and declared, *'Mein Herr, da spricht meine Seele* (Sir, there speaks my soul)', to which the others murmured their assent."

GAS paused for a moment, and then continued,

"I realised that I had been wasting my time with them, so I gave up and returned home to England."

*

As Joshua and I stood surveying the archetypical German landscape from the roof of Hohengeroldseck Castle, I recalled Geoffrey Shepherd's story. I totally understood what he had been trying to convey and, assisted by my knowledge of German nineteenth century literature, how its themes had been stolen, corrupted and evoked by Hitler and his misguided and ultimately wicked followers in order to mesmerise the ordinary German, to seize control of their nation, to wage war and commit genocide. And why many ordinary and otherwise decent Germans had followed them.

I said,

"Joshua, in its way that view is very beautiful, but you know what?"

"No? What?"

"I prefer the hedgerows and thatched cottages of the English countryside any day."

"Oh, Peter, I agree. I would rather look at an Arizonan desert and its beautiful cacti. Because that's home and this isn't."

We were silent for a little while. Then Joshua said,

"But you're not sorry you came, are you?"

"No, not at all, Joshua. I'm very grateful you suggested it and brought me here, although you had been here before."

"It's been a pleasure."

Although I have no specific recollection of it, I would also have visited the Karst Spring in the grounds of the palace. The Karst Spring, or Donaubach, (previous page) is an elaborate and elegant circular terrace, adorned with a monumental marble group statue and surrounding a sunken pool, proclaimed to be the Source of the River Danube, but into which the Breg and Brigath flow.

The following day, I headed back westward. On my way, I may have stayed in the youth hostel in Furtwangen im Schwarzwald. Then, onwards as far as Schönwald im Schwarzwald, and another youth hostel. My hikers' map located the source of the Breg to be close to the tiny, whitewashed St Martin's Chapel (*Martinskappelle*), roofed with pale blue tiles and sporting a slender spire above it. A copyright-protected image of it can be found on Wikipedia.[10] As I approached it, the trees thinned out and, as I was walking up a gentle slope across heathland, I noticed, several yards below and to one side of the path, a metal notice board fixed to a flat stone. Interested, I left the path. The ground dipped slightly and there before me and just below the notice board was an iron pipe sticking out of the ground, with a trickle of water emerging from it that flowed away downhill as a tiny stream. To the best of my recollection, the notice board stated in German,

> Here is the source of the River Danube.
> 100 metres to the west is the watershed
> between Rhine and Danube,
> between North Sea and Black Sea.

A mix of emotions flooded through me: wonder at my presence at so iconic a place; elation at having achieved my goal; and gratitude that I was fit and well and able to rejoice in the moment. I reflected that when it rained, which it wasn't, one hundred metres further up the slope, drops that fell to the west of the ridge above me would eventually find their way almost to England; and those that fell on the other side, would water the coast of Asia. For the romantic youth I then was, that was quite a moment. I hope I would feel much the same in the unlikely event that I find myself at a similar spot again. What I did not appreciate at the time was that it proved to be not just a physical, but the metaphorical, watershed of my stroll through West Germany. That became clear later the same day when, while drinking in an inn back in Schönwald, I fell into conversation with a middle-aged, agreeable and friendly German.

I was so excited by my happening upon the true source of the River Danube that, as I told him about it, my voice ran on and on, articulating uncharacteristically quickly and animatedly. What I did not do, was to introduce myself as English. When I finally dried, my drinking companion smiled and said,

"You are very lucky."

"Yes, I know."

He took a mouthful of beer, swallowed and then,

"*Mein Herr, du bist ein Holländer, Ja* (Sir, you are a Dutchman, Yes)?"

They are words I have never forgotten. Flattered, I replied, in German,

"No, I am not. I am English."

"Are you? Well, you speak German just as if you were a Dutchman."

"Thank you," I replied.

I told him why I had decided to come to Germany and where I had walked. He nodded and our conversation continued along lines that had become all too familiar during my time in Germany. Later that night, when I returned to the youth hostel and went to bed, I reflected upon what he had said. Where was I going to walk to tomorrow? I was running out of places I wanted to see, although I had thought of visiting Titisee, the largest natural lake in the Black Forest. I put out the light and slept. Tomorrow would take care of itself.

*

Grenoble

The next morning at breakfast, I struggled with the option of walking to Titisee. Now that I had achieved my recently adopted goal of visiting the source of the River Danube, the boredom that had already been niggling me and I had been anxious to suppress, returned. My original plan had been to spend eight weeks in Germany, perfecting my spoken German. But, if my fluency in the language was now such that a native German had taken me for a Dutchman, I had achieved that. 'What,' I asked myself, 'is the point of my tramping for another three weeks and possibly another three hundred miles through Germany, when I am so bored and, admit it, Peter, so lonely that I could scream?'

I had been in Germany for five weeks. I decided that I would stay no longer. I was in acute need of culturally familiar company.

Now, patient reader, you may wonder how I had planned to return from Germany to England. Well, now I shall enlighten you. During my final two years in the A-Level Modern Languages set at Westminster, I had become good friends with another member of the set, one Andrew (Andy) Lloyd James. He was seriously bright, far brighter than I, and wonderful company. When he was on form, he was, and still should be, one of the most entertaining people I have ever met. I write, 'still should be', because shortly after 1963, Andy emigrated to Australia, where he forged an amazingly successful career with the Australian Broadcasting Corporation and Australian SBS News. I met him once over lunch in London in the 1970s, but until very recently, we have been out of touch.

An idiosyncratic feature of Andy's presentation was a perpetual tremor affecting both his hands. Early in our friendship, he assured me that it had been like that all his life and betokened no dire health problem.

I have mentioned at page 66 the holidays arranged by Ernst Sanger in 1961 to Mayrhofen and in 1962 to Santander. Andy had been with me on both, which had cemented and deepened our friendship. When I was planning my trip to Germany, Andy was still living in England and had told me that, in April and May of 1963, he was going to spend some weeks in Grenoble, at the end of which his mother would travel to Grenoble and accompany him back home. So, when I suggested to Andy that, when I had completed my walk through West Germany, I should join him in Grenoble and then travel with him and his mother back to England, without demur he agreed. Hence, Andy was expecting me to arrive in Grenoble at the end of May. But now, it was only the end of the first week of that month. There were no mobile phones or internet then and, although I knew the address of the hotel where he would be staying, I did not have its telephone number. I may have sent a postcard, addressed to Andy at that address, warning him that I was planning to arrive three weeks earlier than originally planned, but I have no idea if it arrived. Even if I did and it had done, as events were to prove, he would probably not have read it.

Next, I had to decide how to travel from Schönwald to Grenoble. After enquiring, I caught a bus back to Freiburg and then another bus from Freiburg to Basel. In Basel, I travelled by train, third class on wooden-slatted seats, to Cornavin railway station in Geneva. Cornavin is a hub, connecting with destinations in both Switzerland and France. I bought a ticket to Grenoble. Today, the train takes about three hours from Geneva to Grenoble, and costs £26.22, Standard Class. In 1963 money, that would have been £1.20. I ate dinner in the station restaurant and caught a train that departed at about eight o'clock the same evening.

I arrived three hours later and, by the time I had walked to the address Andy had given me, it was after midnight. The hotel was part of a typical French block of apartments, arranged

Hustings

succeeded him, since when the firm had flourished. He retained both roles until his death in 1974.

One evening, in early November 1956, my father arrived home, opened the front door, stepped inside and exclaimed,

"Disaster! Life as we know it has come to an end!" Or something similar.

It's a long time ago now and I was only twelve years old. I was vaguely aware that the United Kingdom, together with France and Israel, had recently invaded Egypt in an attempt to seize back control of the Suez Canal, which had been nationalised by Gamal Nasser. I was also conscious that the United States was not supporting us, but did not know why, or of the depth of its opposition.

My father was an excellent salesman and understood that, to build a fruitful relationship with a customer, actual or prospective, a display of significant interest in his or her family, political views and the like, was a key to success. As a result, many of my father's customers, drawn largely from royalty, the aristocracy, rich Americans, rich Arabs, politics and business, regarded him as a discreet intimate; someone in whom they could safely confide their innermost thoughts and fears. Earlier on the day that my father had burst into Long Acre so dramatically, Richard Austen Butler, RAB to all and sundry, then MP for Saffron Walden, Lord Privy Seal and Leader of the House of Commons, a customer of Collingwoods and with a reputation for verbal indiscretion, had visited the shop and complained to my father that the United States Navy was sailing its submarines beneath the British naval fleet in Alexandria Harbour in order to sabotage our attempts to depth-charge hostile Egyptian submarines. Whether that was correct or not is not for me to say, but that evening, my father and, by extension, I certainly thought it was. I date my burgeoning interest in politics from that drama-laden disclosure.

The interest stayed with me through my adolescent years, accompanied by growing fascination with the Bar. Biographies of famous barristers, Norman Birkett, Edward Marshall Hall, (in his case three), and F. E. Smith, that currently rest on the bookshelves in my study, provided entertainment and aroused in me more than a little histrionic yearning. I began to imagine myself as both a barrister and a politician.

I became politically active during the 1959 general election, when the leader of the Conservative Party was Harold 'You've never had it so good' Macmillan. The Conservative candidate for Ruislip Northwood was Petre Crowder and I was pressed by my mother into canvassing and delivering his election addresses to households in Eastcote. Even before then, at my mother's behest, I had posted the local Conservative news-sheet through the front doors of loyalists.

Whitehill House, Dane End, Hertfordshire
Painting © Chris Thomas

In the autumn of 1963, my parents, my sister and I moved to Whitehill House, Dane End, Hertfordshire, an imposing part-

Peterborough North Ward Calling Card
© The Author

*

In my papers, there is a letter from Richard Webster, described as 'Hon Secretary Standing Advisory Committee of The National Union of Conservative and Unionist Associations'. The more important an organisation perceives itself, I suppose, the longer the title it adopts. The letter, which is dated 24 July 1972 and had followed an interview in Conservative Central Office, the details of which are lost in my memory, includes the following,

> Your name has been considered by the Standing Committee on Candidates, and I have pleasure in informing you that it has been added to the official list of potential Candidates.

Also amongst my papers are letters from Lord Fitzwilliam and Charles Greenwood, both dated 31 July 1972, expressing delight at my inclusion on the Conservative Party's Candidates List. So far, so good.

I applied to several Conservative Constituency Associations, including Darlington, Small Heath in Birmingham and Loughborough, securing interviews at the last two, but was not selected. Time was marching on and Ted Heath's government was running into serious trouble. After capitulating to the National Union of Miners (NUM) in 1972 over pay, inflation was running at nearly 10 per cent. Mick McGahey, a Scot and fervent communist, had been elected National Vice President of the NUM and was spoiling for a fight to bring down the Conservative Government, as he made clear when he met Ted Heath at Number 10 Downing Street, in November 1973.[4]

In March 1973, I responded to a notice inviting members of the Conservative Party on the Candidates List to apply to become the prospective parliamentary candidate for the Derbyshire constituency of Ilkeston. The result of the June 1970 general election had been,

> R. Fletcher (Labour)....................32,961
> R. Beardsley (Conservative).........15,870
> W. Smit (Liberal)........................6,157
> **Labour majority......................17,091**

Like Peterborough North Ward, the chances of my being elected at Ilkeston were realistically non-existent, but conducting a campaign there would leave me well-placed afterwards, I believed, to secure a safe seat at the following general election. So, I wrote applying and was invited to attend a meeting of the Ilkeston Conservative Party Executive on All Fools' Day, Friday, 1 April 1973.

The parliamentary constituency of Ilkeston then comprised the four industrial and former mining settlements, running south to north, of Ilkeston, Heanor, Ripley and Alfreton. It neighboured the parliamentary constituency of Bolsover, represented in the House of Commons between 1970 and 2019 by Labour's Dennis Skinner, affectionately known then and since as 'The Beast of Bolsover'.

I drove from New Sulehay, Nassington, west of Peterborough, where Mary and I, together with our daughter, Helen, then aged 16 months, had lived since 1972, through Uppingham and Melton Mowbray to Nottingham, turned left at the Queen's Medical Centre and continued under the M1 into Heanor, where I parked outside Heanor Conservative Club and entered. I was directed upstairs to a small, empty room. After a few minutes, a door opened and I was invited into another small room, where about 10 people were sitting, all male, I seem to recall. A short interview took place and then the Chairman, whose name, given what I write about him later, is perhaps fortunately long lost in my memory, asked me,

"Well, Mr Morrell, will you accept our invitation to become our prospective Parliamentary Candidate?"

"Are there no other applicants?"

"No. You're the only one who's applied and we're delighted you have come to see us. Well, young man, what about it?"

A bird in the hand is worth two in the bush!

"Of course!" I declared.

"Good man!"

The *Derby Evening Telegraph* of Wednesday 4 April 1973, reported my selection, adding,

> Mr Morrell, who lives in Northamptonshire, is a solicitor in practice in Peterborough. At present he is treasurer of Peterborough Divisional Conservative Association and chairman of the Political Education Committee. He is married with a 16-month-old daughter. His political interests include tax reform, economic affairs and environmental problems.

> ### YOUTH INTEREST

> Outside politics, he serves on the committees of the Mid-Anglia Association of Youth Clubs and of the Peterborough Society, a body concerned with urban and rural conservation in and around Peterborough and East Northamptonshire. He expects to spend a lot of time in the Ilkeston Division, meeting people and acquainting himself with the particular problems of the constituency. Mr Morrell commented, "I come as a stranger but I hope very soon to be a friend."

I was on my way to the House of Commons, or so I thought.

*

Ilkeston

Whenever I had competed in a rowing regatta, as I had done frequently, rather than dreaming about winning the final, we members of the crew sized up our opponent in the first round. Following my appointment as the Conservative prospective Parliamentary Candidate for Ilkeston, I decided to adopt the same approach. My Labour opponent was Ray Fletcher. Here is the frontispiece of his 1974 election leaflet.

Ray Fletcher's Election Leaflet

Born on 3 December 1921, so 53 years old in February 1974, his full names were Leopold Raymond Fletcher. He served in the British Army between 1941 and 1948 in the Far East, the Middle East and Germany. He became a journalist, author, playwright and lecturer. He first entered Parliament as MP for Ilkeston in 1964 and continued in that role until he retired in 1983.[5] In 1973, he was married to a German aristocratic woman. He told me, when I first met him during the general election campaign in February 1974, that he was fiercely critical of Harold Wilson, who, when Prime Minister between 1964 and 1970, had supported the continued development of the supersonic air-liner, Concorde.[6] It had made its maiden flight on 2 March 1969 and Fletcher considered the project a colossal waste of money, a judgement that was later to prove correct.

Ray Fletcher died on 16 March 1991.[5] According to Masili Mitrokhin, who defected to the UK from Russia in 1992, Fletcher had spied for the Soviets, an allegation fiercely denied by Fletcher's second wife, Catherine, asserting that, in fact, her husband had carried out missions for MI6.

My first contact with Ray Fletcher was following the death of his German wife in late 1973 or early 1974. Upon learning of it, I wrote to Fletcher at the House of Commons. He replied by a letter dated 21 January 1974, thanking me, describing how his wife had many contacts in the Conservative Party and remark-ing,

> When you get here (as you will, though I shall do my best to stop you doing it in Ilkeston!) take my advice: get Mrs Morrell involved in the daily life of Parliament in some way. It will double your effectiveness & halve your burdens. I know.
>
> Yours very sincerely,
> Raymond Fletcher

It was a tone that was very welcome and characterised our relationship during my time as prospective and, later, adopted Conservative Parliamentary Candidate in Ilkeston. It made my task more agreeable than it otherwise might have been and stands in sharp contrast, for example, to the toxic political atmo-sphere in the UK during the recent Brexit saga.

Geoffrey Pool
From election leaflet

My liberal opponent, Geoffrey Pool, aged 33, was a lecturer in geography and environmental studies at the then Leicester College of further Education. I met him only a couple of times during the 1974 campaign and made no personal approach to him. He struck me as a thoroughly decent person, but given the performance of his Liberal predecessor, Mr Smit, who had secured barely 11 percent of the votes in 1970, I chose to pay him scant attention.

*

But all that lay ahead. In April 1973, my priority was to 'nurse' the constituency, forging municipal and business contacts and earning the loyalty and support of local Conservative Party members. And forging is, perhaps, the right word for, in August 1973, I was the guest of Stanton & Staveley Limited at their works in Ilkeston, where, amongst other things, I inspected a newly developed 72 inch plastic matrix pipe, designed to carry liquid under pressure. A poor reproduction overleaf, I'm afraid, but it illustrates the sort of public appearances I made, whilst I nursed the constituency.

Peter Morrell takes a look at Stanton

Author at Stanton Ironworks,
Ilkeston, Nottinghamshire.
Ilkeston Advertiser 24 August 1973

A report of my visit to the since-closed Stanton Ironworks in Ilkeston, accompanied by this photograph, featured in both the local *Ilkeston Advertiser* and the more widely circulating *Derby Evening Telegraph*. After my selection in April 1973, I moved quickly to establish working relationships with the editors of both newspapers that stood me in good stead when the general election was announced the following February.

The Ilkeston Constituency Conservative Association was tiny. The membership of the Executive Committee was in single figures and, whenever I visited an Association event, which I frequently did, those present rarely exceeded a dozen. Since 1922, with the exception of 1931 to 1935, Ilkeston had been represented by Labour Party politicians.

The exception was Abraham Flint, a barrister, who stood for National Labour at the general election in 1931. National Labour candidates were a break-away group of Labour MPs, who chose to support Ramsey MacDonald and the formation of a National Government with the Conservative and Liberal Parties. Flint won from George Oliver, Labour, by two votes.[7] That result remained the smallest majority in any individual constituency election since universal suffrage, until Stephen Gethins won North East Fife for the SNP by two votes in May 2015.[8] Gethins lost the seat at the general election of 2019.[8]

Flint did not stand for re-election in 1935. He continued his career at the Bar and served in the Royal Artillery in the Second World War, rising to the rank of Major. In November 1957, Abraham Flint was made a judge of Circuit No 18 (Nottingham).[7] He died on 23 January 1971.[7]

Returning to my own experience of Ilkeston, like many political associations in a serious minority situation, the Constituency Conservative Association was typically robust. I recall vividly a discussion with its Executive Committee on the topic of capital punishment, which it strongly supported. I have been opposed to it since 1965 or 1966, when I watched a film at an arts cinema in Headington, Oxford, that I continue to believe was a preview of *10 Rillington Place*. The film dramatised the trial and wrongful hanging of Timothy Evans for the murder of his wife. It was later recognised that she had been murdered by Evans' landlord, the notorious mass murderer and necrophiliac, John Christie. *10 Rillington Place* was not generally released until 1971, five years after I had left Oxford University and was married and living and working in the East Midlands.[9]

I voiced my opposition to capital punishment and said that if they did not like it, they could deselect me and find someone else.

"Oh," said the Chairman, "we wouldn't do that, would we?"

He looked around at the others present, who to a man – and they were all men – shook their heads.

"No, we wouldn't," continued the Chairman. "We like you and think you're rather good, so we shall have to agree to disagree, won't we?"

"We shall."

During another meeting of the Executive Committee, the Chairman suggested that I should champion the sending of all African and Asian immigrants in the UK back to the countries from which they originated.

"But," I objected, "what should we do with those who have been born in this country, have British citizenship and whom the country where their parents originated will not accept? What about them?"

The Chairman nodded.

"That's a good point, but we must do something about them."

"Well," I said, "here's a suggestion."

The Chairman's expression brightened.

"Yes?"

"We could build special villages for them and make them live in them."

"That's a good idea."

"But, there's a problem."

"Yes?"

"Some of them might want to live somewhere else, so we should have to make sure they can't leave their village."

"Hmmm." Pause, then, "How should we do that?"

"Well, we could build a high barbed-wire fence around the village, with watch towers along it at intervals and manned by armed guards. How about that?"

The Chairman and the others smiled ruefully. The topic was not raised with me again.

They were a good, loyal bunch, but in a permanently Labour-held seat, they constituted a beleaguered minority and one way of them buoying up their spirits was to adopt attitudes directly contrary to their left-wing opponents. In the political context of those times, when strikes and social breakdown were rife, their reaction was understandable. When the general election was called the following February, both the Ilkeston Conservative Party and its Parliamentary Candidate, needed them and they did not let us down. But, more of that later.

Association events were attended by local Conservative Party members, more often than not, loyal women in their seventies and eighties. When, aged 29, I entered an event venue, I would be treated as if I were a messiah. I understood why and did not let it go to my head, but those occasions revealed within me a hitherto undetected weakness. I had then, and continue to have, a bad memory for names. Faces I can recognise, even if I have only met their owners once, but names? No way and it resulted in embarrassing moments, epitomised by the following imagined, but not untypical, exchange.

I walk into an evening gathering attended as usual by elderly men and women. I approach a woman, whom I recognise from a previous event.

"Ah, Mrs Barber, how lovely to see you."

"Mrs Hind, actually."

"Oh, of course, Mrs Hind. I'm so sorry."

"Not at all, my dear. It's lovely to see you too."

"Thank you. Now, I recall your husband was unwell and in hospital. How is he now?"

"Mr Morrell, I'm afraid my husband died three years ago."

"Oh, I do apologise, Mrs Hind."

"Not to worry, dear."

Something like that happened all too often.

*

Shortly after I had been selected as the Conservative Prospective Parliamentary Candidate for Ilkeston, Conservative Central Office assigned Peter Rost MP to be my mentor. He was then the Member of Parliament for South East Derbyshire. We met and quickly struck up a good relationship and, on several occasions, he invited me to attend debates in the House of Commons, sitting in the Strangers' Gallery. I recall one occasion, when the House was full and Michael Heseltine, then

Minister for Aerospace, delivered a typically flamboyant speech from the Government Front Bench.

Peter Rost continued to represent South East Derbyshire in the House of Commons until the constituency was abolished in 1983, when he was elected Member of Parliament for the newly created constituency of Erewash in Derbyshire, for which he sat until his retirement in 1992.[10]

*

As 1973 wore on, the plight of Ted Heath's government worsened. In October 1973, the Organisation of Arab Petroleum Exporting Countries proclaimed an embargo on exports of oil to nations supportive of Israel in the Yom Kippur War that had started in the same month. Nations targeted included the UK as well as the USA and others. The embargo severely restricted the generation of electricity in the UK because of its effects on transportation and inflation.[11]

At some point during 1973, the national conference of the NUM passed a resolution demanding a pay increase of 35 per cent in defiance of the Government-imposed pay-cap in the public sector, of which the National Coal Board (NCB) formed part. In November 1973, the NUM national executive rejected a pay offer from the NCB and held a national ballot on a strike. It did not pass, but, in place of a strike, the NUM introduced an overtime ban. As most electricity in the United Kingdom was then generated by coal-burning power stations, on 31 December 1973, Ted Heath implemented the Three-Day Week, restricting commercial electricity consumption to three consecutive days each week. Television broadcasts were obliged to finish at 10.30pm and most public houses were closed.[12]

On 24 January 1974, the NUM rejected a pay offer of 16.5 per cent and 81 per cent of its members voted to strike. Speculation that servicemen would be used to transport coal to power stations prompted Mick McGahey to call in a speech for the army to disobey orders and either remain in barracks or join picket lines. That provoked the tabling of an Early Day Motion in the House of Commons condemning him and signed by most, if not all, Conservative MPs and 111 Labour MPs.[12]

The strike began on 5 February and, on Wednesday, 7 February, Ted Heath fired the starting gun. A general election would take place on Thursday, 28 February 1974. I booked a room in the Rutland Hotel, Ilkeston, secured three weeks leave of absence from Greenwoods and on Saturday, 10 February, I bade Mary farewell and turned my Ford Capri northwards, buoyed up by a letter from Igor Judge, now Lord Judge, of whom more later, that had arrived the same morning. It read,

9th February 1974

Dear Peter

Good luck and WIN.

Yours aye,

Igor

*

I now digress from politics to the Law. The reader will recall that my first choice of a legal profession had been the Bar, a choice my father had quashed. He was a strong character and in 1974, in addition to my annual salary of some £2,000 from Greenwoods, I was a director of Collingwoods and in receipt of a director's fee of £1,000 a year. When I was admitted as a solicitor in 1970, £1,000 had been the equivalent of £16,000 in today's money and I had been reluctant to alienate such a source of support. However, by mid-1973, a question mark had arisen over my future.

In January 1972, I had been appointed a salaried partner in Greenwoods and my name appeared at the bottom of the list of partners on the firm's notepaper. The financial structure of Greenwoods then was that equity partners, distinguished from salaried partners, shared the profits of the business amongst themselves, although not all of them equally.

My allocated practice at Greenwoods was in the fields of tax and trusts, but there was very little such work available. Meanwhile, the firm's canny litigation clerk, a retired police serjeant called Fred Hammerton, had spotted my love of the histrionic and had persuaded me to appear as an advocate in local magistrates' courts and the Peterborough County Court. I loved it and received polite plaudits for my performances from fellow professionals.

In 1973, the senior partner and my former principal, Charles Greenwood, called me into his office and offered me a full equity partnership from 1 January 1974. He explained how my share of the profits would be less than the other partners and that, in addition, I would be required to invest a substantial capital sum in the firm. Without going into any more detail, careful analysis of the financial consequences convinced me that it was a poor prospect, and I declined the offer. During the spring and summer of 1973, I looked around for another position as a solicitor and was offered a salaried post by, amongst others, Linklaters, one of the top five law firms in London, an offer I declined. Gradually, I was coming to the conclusion that a career as a solicitor was not for me. So it was that, in September 1973, sunbathing on a beach with Mary in Saint-Tropez, I announced,

"I've decided to go to the Bar."

"What took you so long?" was her response.

Campaign

A MESSAGE FROM
MARY MORRELL

I would like to commend my husband to you as a person who has been and is working extremely hard to get to know the Constituency, its problems, and how they affect the people living and working in it.

As a family man, Peter is aware of how the broader issues of politics affect our daily lives and standard of living, and I can assure you that not only is he concerned with people and their problems, but also he devotes a great deal of his time and energy in thinking about and making an active contribution towards their solution.

In conclusion, he takes his politics very seriously and is just the sort of person we need in Parliament.

Mary Morrell

LABOUR'S U TURN

"One Man's wage increase is another man's price increase"
Harold Wilson Blackburn 8th January, 1970

"If the Government get their law we take the view that that law should be honoured, even if we regard it as unfair. Certainly we would not lend our support to any who would seek by illegal or OTHER MEANS to destroy it."
Harold Wilson B.B.C. 18th January, 1973

"The Labour Party will resolutely support the miners in their efforts ; we shall support the miners"
Tony Benn Heanor, Derbys. 24th December, 1973

"We shall break Phase Three and we shall do all we can to bring the Government down"
Mick McGahey Morning Star 30th Nov., 1973

WHAT A
LABOUR GOVERNMENT
WOULD MEAN TO YOU

"The objectives of the Labour Party require high taxation."
Anthony Crosland Sunday Times 4th April, 1971

"A Labour Government will be an expensive Government with an expensive programme . . . taxes are a certainty."
Roy Hattersley Cambridge 27th May, 1972

"We have to be frank . . . We can no longer pay for higher expenditure just by soaking the rich."
Reg Prentice Socialist Commentary April, 1973

YOU HAVE BEEN WARNED

FOR FAIR BUT FIRM
GOVERNMENT - VOTE
CONSERVATIVE

FIRM BUT FAIR

PETER
MORRELL
CONSERVATIVE

Printed by Keith Moore Printers, South Street, Ilkeston Published by Miss E. M. Patterson, Conservative Office, 30f Bath Street, Ilkeston

Ilkeston Election Address
© *The Author*

Quite early during my nursing of Ilkeston Constituency, I had been informed that, although there was no salaried full-time agent, when a general election was called, the former agent, professionally trained as such, but who had left the constituency to pursue another career when it could no longer afford to pay him, would return to manage my campaign. However, on my arrival in the constituency on Saturday, 10 February, I learnt that the former agent was unwell and would not, after all, be participating in the campaign. By law, I had to have an agent, so who was it to be?

Miss E. M. Patterson, 'Pat' to all and sundry, was a member of the Conservative Association. Hailing from Northern Ireland, she was a formidable character in her sixties, unmarried and plagued by a chronic heart disorder, which slowed our progress on foot up and down the hills in the four towns in the constituency. She turned out to be a star, supporting me every inch of the way, laughing and growling with me, when circumstances warranted.

The first thing to do was to register my name as the Conservative candidate. The next, was to prepare my election address (previous page).

*

When I arrived in Ilkeston on Saturday, 10 February, 1974, my experience of previous general election campaigns led me to ask where, when and by whom would house-to-house canvassing be done. The answer was there would be no canvassing. There simply were not enough willing and available helpers. I was assured that three or four Party members would stuff my election address into envelopes, which, courtesy of Royal Mail, would be delivered to every household in the constituency, but that was all the help there would be.

So, how was I going to publicise myself? The plan I devised, with Pat's wholehearted approval, was that I would hold a public meeting in the constituency every weekday evening from Monday to Friday. On the two Saturdays of the campaign, I would conduct walkabouts in the market squares of the four towns that comprised the constituency; so, Ilkeston and Heanor on Saturday 16 February and Ripley and Alfreton on Saturday 23 February. On Saturday afternoons, I would drive home and return to resume campaigning on Monday mornings. Mary made me a blue rosette, 10 inches in diameter, which graced my jacket throughout the campaign. At every weekday meeting, I would deal with a different, but relevant topic, having issued a 300-word press release to the local newspapers, the *Ilkeston*

Advertiser, the *Ripley and Heanor News* and the *Derby Evening Telegraph*. I arranged early meetings with the editors of all three and was delighted with their interest in my campaign plan and the policies I endorsed. The details of the campaign, the dates, times and places of appearances, were advertised in full-page spreads in the *Ilkeston Advertiser* and the *Ripley and Heanor News*. When I was not holding a meeting or present in a town square, I toured the constituency in my Ford Capri, equipped with a roof-mounted loudspeaker, announcing who I was. Name recognition would be vital when electors went into voting booths on 28 February.

The newspapers came up trumps. Every one of my press releases was reproduced word-for-word, with each newspaper supplying its own catchy headline. It mattered not that the meetings were poorly attended, usually by between five and ten elderly supporters and the odd small dog, but from early on, there was almost always a self-proclaimed Trotskyist at the back, who heckled,

"What does a public school, privileged bloke like you know about the working-class voters in this constituency?"

He was a godsend and I conducted lively debates with him, the swivelling heads of my elderly, mainly female supporters following the exchanges as if they were spectators at the Wimbledon All England Lawn Tennis Championships.

On Friday, 15 February, during a visit to Derby to meet the editor of the *Derby Evening Telegraph*, I received an unexpected boost to my campaign of raising public awareness of who I was. After leaving the newspaper's offices, I was walking up a long, straight, gently sloping road, when, several hundred yards ahead of me, I saw two adolescent girls running towards me, pursued by a police constable in full uniform, holding his helmet under an arm. Did I step aside to let them pass? I did not! I placed myself firmly in the path of one of the girls, who collided with me, causing both my arms to encircle her. As I held onto her, her companion, who had stopped to help, was seized by the police constable.

"Thank you, Sir."

"Not at all," I replied. "Glad to have been of help," and I told him who I was.

As he marched the two girls off, I returned to the offices of the *Derby Evening Telegraph* and reported what had happened. It ran a news item on it on the following Monday, but better still, the editor had syndicated the item and the following appeared in the national *Daily Express* the next day.

Vote hunter joins in chase

Vote-catching Tory candidate Peter Morrell joined a police chase yesterday to catch two girls trying to escape.
Later he gave a speech in his Ilkeston, Derby, constituency on law and order.

I could not have wished for better!

Occasionally during the campaign, I would be asked, together with my opponents, Ray Fletcher and Geoffrey Pool, to participate in studio debates, broadcast by *BBC Radio Derby*. It was on one of those occasions when Ray Fletcher demonstrated significant kindness towards me. Conservative Central Office had written to every Conservative candidate with a list of those Labour MPs, who had failed to sign the Early Day Motion condemning Mick McGahey for his call to the army to mutiny if it were ordered to transport coal to power stations. Central Office had requested in the letter that if the Labour candidate in the constituency, for which the recipient was standing, had omitted to put his or her name to it, the recipient should publicise that in the local press. Ray Fletcher's name was not on the list, so I dutifully wrote a letter to the *Ilkeston Advertiser*, pointing this out and condemning his failure to put his name to the motion. The day before the next weekly issue of the newspaper was due to hit the streets, I met Ray Fletcher and Geoffrey Poole at *BBC Radio Derby* studios. As a matter of courtesy, I told Ray what I had done.

He glared at me.

"Peter, you have made a terrible mistake. On the day that motion was laid before the House of Commons, I was attending my wife's funeral. The House rose the next day, so I had no opportunity to sign it, which I would have done."

I was horrified.

"Oh, Ray, I'm so sorry."

"If that letter is published, I'll crucify you."

As soon as I left the studios, I rang the editor of the *Ilkeston Advertiser* from a telephone box and explained what had happened. The editor assured me the letter would not be published and, true to his word, it was not.

I recall another occasion at *BBC Radio Derby*, when Ray took me gently to one side and said,

"Peter, you're not going to win here. You know that, don't you."

"Of course I do, Ray."

"But you're a promising lad. The House of Commons needs young blood like you. You'll go far and I'm sure you'll be chosen for a safe Conservative seat at the next general election."

"Thank you, Ray."

"But, Peter, always remember this!"

"Yes?"

Ray glanced towards Pool,

"We must keep the bloody Liberals out!"

BBC Radio Derby was conducting live debates with the candidates for each Derbyshire constituency, inviting electors to submit questions for the candidates to answer. Pat told me about it and the date when the Ilkeston candidates were scheduled to appear. An idea occurred to me.

"Pat, I am going to draft a letter designed to put Ray Fletcher on the spot and send to *BBC Radio Derby*."

"Oh, but Peter, that's no good. They'll see it's from you and ignore it."

"Yes, but it won't be from me."

"What do you mean?"

"We'll get a member of the Association to write what I draft and send it in under his or her name."

Looking back on it, now that I am forty-seven years older, I am reminded of a remark, reputed to have been made by Francis Bacon, that youth and discretion are ill-wed companions. But we did it and when the three of us, Fletcher, Pool and I, were sitting in the studio with the presenter and the show went live, the presenter said,

"Well, unfortunately, we have only received one letter from the electors of Ilkeston." He read it out and remarked, "It seems like it's one for you, Mr Fletcher."

I spent the remaining half hour or so of the programme putting Ray on the defensive – successfully, I recall. It may well have been afterwards that he made the remark to me just quoted above.

Am I proud of it now? I am not, but, at the time, it was fun and deeply satisfying.

*

After a while, I found addressing poorly attended meetings night after night depressing. They had a good purpose, as I have explained, but at times, it was hard pounding, so imagine my delight when, one day when I returned to the small Conservative Association office that was the campaign headquarters, someone said to me,

"Peter, please could you ring this number. It's an election agent who wants to talk to you."

When I dialled the number, the telephone was answered by Ken Clarke's agent in Rushcliffe, at that time, the strongest Conservative constituency in the country. I had met Ken and his wife, Gillian, now sadly deceased, during my nursing of Ilkeston the previous year.

"Peter, would you be free this evening to come to Rushcliffe and keep a meeting warm for Ken? He's been held up at *BBC Radio Birmingham* studios and will be about half-an-hour late."

"Look, I've got a meeting arranged here this evening. I'll see if we can cancel it and ring you back."

We could and I did.

"Great!" came the response. He gave me directions to the venue. "The meeting starts at eight. Can you be here by half seven?"

"I'll be there."

"Good man!"

After all the intervening years, with no newspaper report to refresh my memory, my recall of the evening is patchy. What I do remember is that that the event took place in a huge hall, packed with about 300 of Ken's supporters, to whom I unashamedly pandered, rolling out all the old saws dear to Conservative loyalists' hearts and evoking round upon round of enthusiastic applause. I also recall Ken appearing at the back of the hall, his features betraying consternation at my irresponsible performance. I swiftly brought my part to a close and announced Ken's arrival to the ecstatic crowd. Oh, what an evening it was! It was like drinking fine claret instead of *vin ordinaire*.

Kenneth Clarke continued to represent Rushcliffe until he announced that he would not fight the general election of December 2019. In September 2020, he was created Baron Clarke of Nottingham.

*

Ilkeston, Heanor, Ripley and Alfreton are in what was formerly mining country. There had been a number of collieries in the constituency: Manners, Oakwell and Peacock in Ilkeston, Shipley Coppice in Heanor, Highfield in Alfreton and Ripley Colliery in the town of that name. By 1974 all had closed, some many years previously. In 2011, a proposal by UK Coal to extract 750,000 tons of coal from the Lodge House open cast site in Ilkeston was approved in the face of local opposition. The project failed when, in 2015, UK Coal went into liquidation and, by 2018, there was a more appropriate plan to develop the whole site as a nature reserve.[13]

In 1974, however, there remained a strong mining tradition in the constituency. Many of the men still worked in nearby collieries and, amongst some, support for the NUM was firm.

However, there was also simmering resentment of mineworkers amongst other residents, whose sympathies were with the Government in its dispute with the NUM. I was told more than once that during and in the years immediately following the Second World War, whilst there was much poverty in the area, mineworkers were paid so extravagantly to deter them from striking, that it was not uncommon for them to go to work at their colliery in taxis.

My planned walkabouts offered a rare opportunity to meet local folk who were not members or supporters of the Conservative Party. In Ripley Market Place on Saturday 15 February 1974, a middle-aged, working-class woman approached me, took in my outsize blue rosette and remarked,

"So, you're the Conservative Candidate, are you?"

"Good morning, Madam. Yes, I am."

"Well, I've never voted Conservative before, but I am this time. I'm going to vote for you."

"Thank you very much. But tell me, please, why the change of heart?"

"Well, my old man's a working miner." She mentioned a neighbouring pit in Derbyshire where he was employed and continued, "So, I know all about the National Union of Miners and that Arthur Scargill. My old man tells me. Reds under the beds they are. Bloody reds!"

In 1974, Arthur Scargill, a dedicated left-wing socialist, had been elected president of the Yorkshire Miners' Association, an ally of the NUM, which, in 1994, would be amalgamated with it.[14] Together with Mick McGahey, Scargill was playing a major role in the confrontation between the NUM and Ted Heath's Government, as he did again 10 years later, during the 1984 miners' strike, in the NUM's battle with Margaret Thatcher's government.

A memorable moment in the campaign occurred when I suggested to Pat that we should visit the Alfreton Miners' Welfare Club. At least, that's how locals then referred to it, although a search online reveals that, although there are a number of miners' welfare clubs in Alfreton, none of them are called by that name today. In any event, the one I decided to visit had the reputation of being the venue most favoured by working miners in Alfreton and it was where I was likely to meet local miner leaders.

"Oh, Peter!" Pat exclaimed, in her strong Ulster accent, "you canna go there. They'll morder you!"

"Listen Pat," I said patiently, "if I am elected as the Member of Parliament in this constituency …" I chose to ignore her faintly scornful expression, "… I shall not just be representing the people who voted for me, but everyone in the constituency, regardless of their political views."

"Yes, but …"

"No, Pat. I assure you I can look after myself and if you would rather not come as well, then that'll be fine by me."

"Of course I'll come with you!" she retorted indignantly.

Our visit was arranged for the second Saturday during the campaign, following my marketplace walkabouts. We arrived at the club shortly after 12 noon. After entering the Club and introducing ourselves at the desk in the foyer, we were directed to a door opposite the entrance from the street. Sporting, as always, my 10-inch blue rosette and followed by Pat, I opened the door and walked into a large room with a bar along one side of it. The room was packed with men sitting at round tables. There was a large table in the middle of the room and smaller tables around its periphery. As we approached the bar, the room fell silent. A candidate was and is not permitted by electoral law to buy a drink, or anything else for that matter, for any voter in the constituency, so Pat ordered me half a pint of bitter. As I was raising it to my lips, a tall, heavily-built man detached himself from the large round table in the middle of the room and approached. Towering above me, he said,

"Now then, young man," he glanced down at my rosette, "happen you're the Conservative candidate, yes?"

"Yes, I am."

"Well, you'd better come and sit down and give an account of yourself."

He motioned towards the big round table. Two chairs were empty. One was his and the other had been vacated to accommodate me. We sat down and, for the next half hour, I was grilled, not just by the leader who had initially spoken to me, but by the others round the table. They were intelligent and articulate. Adopting a cricketing metaphor, I saved my wicket and, along the way, scored the odd single, but no boundaries.

Finally, the big man brought it to a close.

"Well, thank you, lad, for chatting with us. You'll do all right, but we won't be voting for you, will we lads?"

He looked round at his companions, all of whom gently shook their heads.

"You see, lad, we're all Labour here, aren't we lads?"

Again, the look around at the circle of nodding heads. And then,

"But you know what's wrong with this country, don't you, lad?"

"Well, I believe I do, otherwise I wouldn't be standing for Parliament, but what do you think?"

"What do I think? There's too much bloody social security, that's what I think."

His companions nodded their agreement. It was intended as a parting shot, so I decided not to engage. I thanked them for their time and, together with Pat, who had stayed at the bar, we left.

"Did you hear that, Pat?"

"I did. I thought you did very well."

"But what about his closing remark? Did you hear that?"

"I did, Peter."

"They're just as Conservative as we are."

"They are, but they'll not vote for you."

"I know that, Pat. I know that."

I have never forgotten my visit to the Alfreton Miners' Welfare Club and, in particular, the big miner's closing remark. I remembered it especially on 13 December 2019, when the results of the general election were broadcast, with the news that Boris Johnson's Conservative Party had breached Labour's Red Wall in the Midlands and North of England. There's more that unites than divides us, as the Labour MP, Jo Cox, reminded the House of Commons in her maiden speech on 3 June 2016, thirteen days before she was murdered by Thomas Mair in her constituency of Batley and Spen.

*

I now pray the reader's forbearance once again, because, to make sense of the result of the 1974 general election, it is necessary to explore a little contextual history.

Labour, led by Harold Wilson, won the general election in 1964 with a majority of four and in 1966 with a majority of 98. Between 1964 and 1970, Wilson's government broadly continued the post-war consensus of the State exercising considerable power over the nation's industrial affairs, including the setting of levels of pay in both the public and private sectors, as it had done during the Second World War. However, consequent inefficiencies were becoming increasingly apparent and, long before 1970, the UK had earned itself the sobriquet abroad, 'Sick Man of Europe'. Its economic performance had fallen behind those, for example, of Germany and France. A radical rethink was called for and this took place during a conference held by Ted Heath and the Conservative Shadow Cabinet at the Selsdon Park Hotel in January 1970. Inflation was an ongoing problem and considerable attention had been paid to its causes. A group of Conservative thinkers, led by Keith Joseph, concluded that the economics pioneered by John Maynard Keynes were no

R. Fletcher (Labour).....................31,500
P. Morrell (Conservative).............17,320
G. Pool (Liberal).........................11,734
Labour majority........................14,180

Geoffrey Pool and I had reduced Ray Fletcher's majority by 2,900. What is fascinating about the general election of February 1974 is that every constituency that was directly associated with coal mining swung to the Conservatives, whilst all the others swung Labour. In Ilkeston, the swing in my favour was the second highest in the United Kingdom. I later learnt that, at Conservative Central Office, my name had been marked as a 'blue chip'.

So, not such a bad result for me after all.

*

A Parliamentary Encounter

Palace of Westminster
Photo © Image by luxstorm from Pixabay

In 1990, after four years sitting as an Assistant Recorder without mishap or embarrassment to HM The Queen, whose Coat of Arms graces the wall above every judicial bench, I progressed to the office of Recorder. Recorders also sit part-time. Then, in October 1991, I received a letter from John Heritage, Head of the Judicial Appointments Group at the Lord Chancellor's Department, inviting me to attend for an interview in the House of Lords, with a view to appointment as a Circuit Judge.

Possibly the second most important person in a barrister's life after his or her spouse, whose support is invaluable, is the senior clerk of the set of chambers from which the barrister practises. When I was at the Bar, barristers in a set of chambers were not in a relationship of partnership, unlike, for example, solicitors or accountants or general practitioners. The same is true today, although, for several years, practising barristers have been permitted to be employed as advocates by firms of solicitors, by the Crown Prosecution Service and in other salaried posts. In the set of chambers in which I was a tenant, a barrister paid a monthly rent towards the cost of administering the set, but whatever was earned in excess of that was the barrister's to keep. The barrister's practice was managed, arranged, call it what you will, by the clerks. The clerks market- ed their barristers and, when a brief to appear in court arrived in chambers, they allocated it to the member of chambers whom they judged was best suited to act as the advocate in the case. In time, a barrister would build a reputation and assemble a loyal cadre of solicitors, who would brief him or her in preference to others in the set. But if the barrister chosen by an instructing solicitor was not available to conduct the case, the clerks would select a substitute, agree the choice with the instructing solicitor and pass the brief to the substitute. Thus was a barrister's practice built and sustained. A barrister in private practice was not permitted to negotiate his or her fee. That was the role of the clerks. Hence the senior clerk, in charge of the other clerks, was absolutely central to the professional success or otherwise of the tenant. I imagine similar arrangements prevail today.

In 1991, Chris Owen was the senior clerk in the set of chambers from which I practised. Capable, efficient and author- itarian, he was the most important person in my professional life. I first consulted Mary, who approved of my decision to seek appointment as a Circuit Judge, but what about Chris Owen? His reaction would be as important.

"I don't think you should, Boss," he pronounced, using the moniker he used for all his charges. "You're in line for silk."

He meant, for appointment as a QC. In those days, the names of new QCs, appointed by the Queen on the advice of the Lord Chancellor, who in 1991 was James MacKay, were announced every Maundy Thursday.

"The problem, Chris," I explained, "is that James MacKay has let it be known that he will not appoint a silk as a judge until the silk has been in post and successful for at least five years. If I am made a silk next Easter, I shall be nearly forty-eight and hence not eligible for appointment to the Circuit Bench until I am fifty-three. To qualify for a full judicial pension, I should

Why?

I was called to the Bar in 1974. I practised as a barrister until I was appointed to the Circuit Bench on 11 March 1992. I led, as I do now, a regular life, living in a relatively isolated rural situation, shooting, fly-fishing, socialising and generally fitting the stereotype of a public school- and Oxbridge-educated, professional, white, middle-class male.

On 6 July 2008, aged 64, I was ordained an Anglican deacon in Peterborough Cathedral and, a year later, on 4 July 2009, an Anglican priest in the same cathedral.

Peterborough Cathedral
Photo © The Author

Since then, I have ministered as such, leading worship, conducting baptisms, marriages and funerals and engaging in pastoral care where I live in North East Northamptonshire and in the Costa Blanca in Spain, where, as already mentioned, Mary and I have a holiday home.

I retired from the Circuit Bench on 25 May 2009, my sixty-fifth birthday and thirty-four days before my ordination as priest. During my last week of sitting as a Circuit Judge, judges, advocates and court staff attended before me successively in Leicester and Northampton Crown Courts to bid me farewell. Kind words were said about me and then it was my turn to respond. I did so, thanking everyone for their kindness and support over the years. On both occasions, I concluded with,

"On my retirement as a judge, I draw comfort that I shall have a better chance of getting to heaven as a priest than I would have done as a judge, as this little tale illustrates.

A young couple much in love, are both killed in a road accident in the week before they are due to be married. As they reach the pearly gates, Saint Peter greets them.

'Hello. It's wonderful to welcome you. We're desperately short of young people here. Is there anything I can do for you?'

The two glance shyly at one another and then the young man says,

'Well, Sir, we're very much in love and we were about to be married when we were killed.'

'Yes, we know that.'

'So, we have a request, please.'

'Yes?'

'Is there any chance of being married up here?'

Saint Peter frowns.

'Well, I've never been asked that before. Sit down and I'll go and see what I can arrange.'

The young couple sit and, inasmuch as time passes in heaven, it passed. After a little while, the man turns to his fiancée and says,

'You know how much I love you, don't you?'

'Of course, I do,' she replies. 'Me too.'

'Yes, well, have you thought about this? Down there, marriage is for life, but up here it's for ever. Now, not for one moment do I believe that anything will go wrong, but just in case, I think we should ask about getting a divorce up here. What do you think?'

After a short pause, she sighs and replies,

'Yes, I suppose you're right.'

Saint Peter returns, holding a clipboard and looking pleased with himself.

'It's all arranged,' he announces happily. 'You can be married in heaven.'

'That's wonderful, Sir,' says the man and then, more quietly, 'but, just in case it doesn't work, can we get a divorce in heaven?'

Saint Peter throws the clipboard to the ground and exclaims,

'Look, it's taken me this long to find a priest up here. How much longer do you think it's going to take me to find a judge?'"

Appropriately, my departure from the Bench was marked by laughter. On 20 May 2009, the day following the farewell ceremony at Northampton Crown Court, the *Northampton Chronicle and Echo* reported on my retirement with a full page spread, headed *'I have a better chance of Heaven as a priest!'* and featuring a photograph of me in judicial robes, taken against a backdrop of leather-bound law reports, together with my biographical details and a digest of kind remarks from fellow judge, Charles Wide QC, and barrister, Michael Ellis, later Member of Parliament for Northampton North, a QC, Solicitor General and, since 2 March 2021, Attorney General in Boris Johnson's Government.

From time to time, people have asked me why I decided to be an Anglican priest. Using that well-worn cliché: What had been my journey? In the interests of social ease I used to deflect those requests, as it's quite a long story, but I have now decided to tell it.

*

Dawning

When I was very young, neither my mother nor my father was a churchgoer. However, before I was sent in May 1952, aged nearly eight, to board at Orley Farm Preparatory School, in South Harrow, Middlesex, I had regularly attended Sunday School at St Martin's Church, Ruislip.

During term-time at Orley Farm, as well as weekday morning assemblies consisting, from memory, of prayers, a reading from Scripture and a hymn, every Sunday, all pupils attended Morning Prayer according to the Book of Common Prayer, alternating between the school gym, where it was led by Jack Ellis, the headmaster, and St Mary's Church, Harrow-on-the-Hill, conducted by the parish priest. During school holidays, I did not attend worship. Nor were prayers said at home.

In the autumn of 1957, I left Orley Farm and started at Westminster School. During the five years I spent there, the whole school, with the exception of three Roman Catholic boys, but including the Jewish pupils, attended an act of worship every weekday, including Saturdays, in Westminster Abbey. It started at 9am and lasted some 15 minutes. Lessons began at 9.30am. Worship included a canticle, prayers and two hymns, the latter accompanied by the Abbey's magnificent organ, occasionally played by Sir William McKie, who had been the organist at the Coronation in June 1953, but, more often, by one of his students. Worship was always led either by the headmaster, John Dudley Carleton, or by his deputy, styled 'The Under Master', Henry Christie, both of whom would be robed in the red cassock customarily worn in Royal Peculiars, as Westminster Abbey was and remains.

Meanwhile, although neither my parents attended Sunday worship, I started to do so at St Lawrence Church, Bridle Road,

Eastcote, a two-minute walk from Long Acre. In common with most of the nearby dwellings dating from the 1930s, the church is brick-built and spacious, with a broad nave and two generous side aisles. The worship, when I attended, was Anglo-Catholic, or High Church as it is sometimes termed, instilling in me a love for that style of liturgy that has remained.

I recall also attending Holy Trinity Church in Northwood for a while, because somewhere I had met the very pretty daughter of its incumbent. We were of the same age and became good friends. Time spent together after worship, alone in the wood behind the church, became a regular and pleasant Sunday activity. Sadly, I do not recall her name. If she reads this, I wish her well and hope that life has treated her kindly.

On 16 March 1959, aged 14, I was confirmed in Westminster Abbey, although for reasons that need not detain the reader, I did not receive Holy Communion until some years later.

It was either in my penultimate or final year at Westminster that an event occurred that, although I did not realise it at the time, was to put me on course for a much closer association with Christianity and the Church of England. At the morning office, pupils sat in the Abbey by houses. Mine was Ashburnham and, on the occasion I describe, we were sitting in the North Transept. Outside, it was summer, but cloudy. Suddenly, a narrow shaft of sunlight pierced the rose window opposite me in the South Transept, scythed almost vertically through the semi-gloom and illuminated those sitting beneath. It was a numinous moment, conveying to me that, significant though I believed human beings to be, there was someone else even more important. Someone of overwhelming power had entered the Abbey and spoken to me personally. Years later, I realised that when God speaks to us, he does not use a telephone.

As anyone reading this will readily grasp, that moment remains with me.

In January 1963, as I recount at page 6, I secured a place at University College, Oxford and after the walk in West Germany that I describe in **Wandervogel** and a tour around Italy in July and August of the same year with three school-friends in my 1948 Standard 8, Flying Tourer that boasted a safe top speed of 55mph, in the October I matriculated, as it is styled, at Oxford University.

During my first year at Oxford, my attendance at University College Chapel was patchy, mainly because the Sunday service of Holy Communion occurred quite early and, with a fair cargo of alcohol on board, I generally only reached my bed in College in the early hours of the morning. Many a Sunday morning it was from between the sheets that I heard the chapel bell calling College members to worship. Poor academic performance consigned me to lodgings outside College during my second and third years at Oxford, thus averting the feelings of guilt that the calling bell had previously aroused in me. Nevertheless, I did manage to attend Chapel occasionally.

Whenever I was at home in Hertfordshire, I attended worship in two local churches, All Saints, Little Munden (overleaf), situated on a hill above Dane End next to the headquarters of Reuters UK, and St Catherine's, in nearby Sacombe.

As happened with me, my suspicion is that a number of folk acquire the habit of Sunday worship as children, maintain it through adolescence and then abandon it in early adulthood. Some return to it, as I did. Others, sadly do not. By the time of my marriage on 6 June 1970, my Sunday church attendance was routine.

Mary lived with her parents and brother, Ian, in the Old Rectory, Paston, once a village but, by 1970, a suburb on the northern edge of Peterborough. It was a fine old house, some of it dating from the 13th century. Sadly, it was badly damaged in a fire some years later. It has been rebuilt, preserving its exterior appearance, but comprising two separate dwellings within.

All Saints Church, Little Munden, Hertfordshire
Photo © Julian Osley (cc-by-sa/2.0)

The Old Rectory was immediately next to All Saints Church, Paston, where we were to be married and the reception was planned to take place in my parents-in-law's garden, the guests walking to it from the church. The incumbent, the Reverend Sidney Cuthbertson, was a good friend of Mary's parents, which gave the whole ceremony a relaxed and slightly intimate flavour. Mary was and is not confirmed, so we did not have a nuptial mass. The marriage ceremony was fixed for three o'clock in the afternoon and Sidney granted my request to be given Holy Communion alone by him in the morning. The day

Initiation

Apethorpe lies about two miles from the rural hamlet that is New Sulehay. Today, New Sulehay comprises three dwellings and the premises of R J Sutton Engineering, a modest but highly successful and busy engineering business. Apethorpe is a settlement with a fascinating history. Again, this is not the place to expound upon that in detail, but, if the reader is interested, he or she should Google 'Apethorpe' and 'Apethorpe Palace'.

Apethorpe Palace, Northamptonshire
Photo © Baroness von Pfetten

To understand why John Humphries had fallen out with Apethorpe Church, however, some background is required. Apethorpe is a small village, and in 1991, which is when I am writing about, it was home to some one hundred residents. Apethorpe Hall, now renamed Apethorpe Palace,[2] the property of Jean Christophe Iseux, Baron von Pfetten zu St. Mariakirchen, is an important heritage building. Currently, it is undergoing restoration under the professional supervision of Baron von Pfetten's wife, Nadia, a conservation architect, who hails from a line of Venetian architects.[3]

Until Tudor times, Apethorpe Palace, together with the village and an extensive surrounding estate, was the property of the Crown. From 1551, it was owned successively by the Mildmay and Fane families. In 1904, it was bought by Sir Henry Brassey, later 1st Baron Brassey of Apethorpe.[4] The Palace and 70 acres, but not the rest of the estate, were sold by the Brassey family after the Second World War.[2] The family had moved from Apethorpe Hall into the substantial and elegant 18th century Apethorpe Manor House before the war and, in 1991, it was the home of Lord David and Lady Caroline (Midgie) Brassey, with both of whom Mary and I became good friends.

In 1991, there was a faintly feudal character to Apethorpe and an impression that the Brassey family regarded St Leonard's Church as akin to a private chapel. David was the patron, but neither he nor Midgie was unpleasant about it, quite the contrary, but their sense of proprietorship tended to influence their approach towards others in, or associated with, the village. Midgie, together with Marjorie Blake, was churchwarden. The falling-out with the vicar had occurred in 1990. Midgie told me that she and Humphries, who held strong left-wing convictions that she did not share, simply did not get on. One day, after celebrating Holy Communion in Apethorpe, Humphries announced to Midgie in the porch of St Leonard's that he would never lead worship there again. In so many words, Midgie told him she was pleased. Shortly afterwards, when the then Bishop of Peterborough, Bill Westwood of BBC fame, informed Midgie that, as a result, he was going to close the church, she retorted, rightly or wrongly, that he did not have the authority to do so. It remained open. From then, until the appointment as priest-in-charge of Bishop John Flack in 2008, retired clergy were engaged by Midgie and Marjorie to hold regular Holy Communion services on Sundays.

When I first attended a service there, I liked it. As all services in a small settlement should be, its liturgy was, and remains to this day, middle-of-the-road, so as not to alienate worshippers from differing traditions. On that Sunday in 1991, there were a dozen or so present in church and the impression I gained was that they were determined to 'go it alone' and keep Christian worship in Apethorpe alive and well. That appealed to me. I have a reasonable singing voice and thought that I could make a useful contribution, so I began to attend every Sunday, always sitting in the pew farthest from the front.

Seven years later, in July 1998, the following exchange between Midgie and me occurred, probably in Apethorpe Manor House.

"Peter?"

"Yes, Midgie."

"Peter, next Sunday, none of our regulars will be here to take Holy Communion, so I want you to lead Morning Prayer."

"Oh, No, Midgie! That's not why I come to Apethorpe Church."

"Peter!" Her tone was admonitory and authoritative. "Next Sunday, you will take Morning Prayer."

I know when I'm beaten.

"All right, Midgie, then I shall."

"Thank you."

"But I'm not allowed to preach a sermon. You know that."

Lay people are not authorised by Canon Law to preach sermons.

"I do know that, but you can give a talk, like ..." she mentioned an Apethorpe resident, who sometimes stepped into the breach, "... does, whenever he takes a service."

So it was that, on Sunday 26 July 1998, I led worship in church for the first time. Despite a lifetime of public speaking, a feeling of unworthiness gripped me as, during the singing of the opening hymn, I walked up the nave from the west end of St Leonard's to the leader's desk. Who did I think I was to perform such a role? However, after I reached the desk and, at the conclusion of the hymn, turned to welcome the congregation, self-assurance returned, buoyed by the reflection that I had neither bargained for, nor offered to take the service. It had been Midgie who, in her wisdom, had chosen me. As events have transpired, her judgement was not wide of the mark. God does not use a telephone.

On that occasion, it was Morning Prayer according to the Book of Common Prayer, a service that I loved then and still do. I can fix the date, because the talk I gave is stored on my laptop and is reproduced at **Appendix A**. I was and remain fascinated by Spain in general and by the legend of St James the Greater and Santiago de Compostela in particular. I knew a good deal about it, so I was delighted to give the talk I did. But, at 2,217 words, it was far too long, and I marvel at the patience of those present that they did not walk out or tell me to shut up.

Galloping through the next few years, I became increasingly involved in worship at St Leonard's, Apethorpe. I was appointed an altar server and led non-sacramental worship when no ordained clergy were available. The regulars were the Reverend Canon Michael McAdam, one-time Chaplain to the Bishop of London, next Vicar of Much Hadham in Hertfordshire and, after he moved to Barnwell, Northamptonshire, Rural Dean in the Oundle Deanery for a year before he retired; the Reverend Bill Shire; and the Reverend Albert Irwin, one-time Vicar of St Martin's, Stamford, the church of the Marquesses of Exeter. Whether they concerted their approach, I know not, but after a while each of them separately suggested to me that I should put myself forward for ordination.

Not for one moment, I truthfully assure the reader, had that thought occurred to me. However, I was flattered and, upon the premise that, if and when God calls you to his service, as I thought he might have called me, you are duty-bound to respond, in late 2000, I made an appointment to see the Reverend Canon Bill Croft, then the Diocesan Director of Ordinands (DDO). Today in the Diocese of Peterborough, the person charged with the responsibility of acting as the sieve, through which aspirant clergy may or may not be permitted to pass, is styled the Director of Ordinands Vocation and Formation Team Leader.

*

I met Bill Croft in the Peterborough Cathedral Deanery in the following February. It was very cold outside and barely warmer within. It matters not why at this distance, but Croft was not then convinced my vocation was sufficiently strong. There was also a sense that we never properly engaged, but were talking at cross purposes. At all events, he told me that I was not suitable and I left.

In 1997, Mary and I bought the house in Spain (see pages 232 and 233 *post*) and, pandemic permitting, I go there every spring, which occurs earlier in Spain than in England. Whilst there in February and March 2001, I reflected on the situation and decided that the only step open to me, if I wished to respond to what I still believed might have been God's call, was to become a reader.

For those unfamiliar with the post, a reader is a theologically trained minister in the Church of England, who is not admitted to one of the ecclesiastical orders of deacon, priest and bishop, but is authorised to lead worship and preach. A licensed reader may also conduct baptisms and funerals, but may not consecrate the bread and wine used at Holy Communion. A reader may also not conduct a marriage, because, in civil law, a reader is not a Registrar of Marriages, as all ordained Anglican clergy in England automatically are.

When Mary and I returned from Spain, a letter from Croft awaited me, in which he apologised for the misunderstandings that had arisen during our meeting and invited me to see him again. I did so at the end of March on a rather warmer day. He repeated his apology, which I accepted, and suggested that I should consider applying to be licensed as a reader. Since that was what I had already decided to do, we parted on a happy note.

I was accepted for reader training, which lasted three years, during which I was authorised to preach and did so on many Sundays in St Leonard's Church, Apethorpe. On 14 May 2005, I was licensed as a reader in a ceremony in Peterborough Cathedral, after which, in addition to preaching sermons, I regularly led non-sacramental worship at Apethorpe.

*

It was during the journey to South Devon that I began to entertain doubts about the wisdom of hiring the minibus I was driving. Anyone who has driven the M5 between Bristol and Exeter will recall a relatively level road, with no steep climbs. The minibus, however, laboured up the gentlest incline and I feared for our drive over the Picos de Europa, the relatively high range of mountains in Northern Spain that lies between Santander and León. The weather was fine and dry.

We spent an agreeable evening with Liz and Mike in Lisburne Farm and the next morning, following the taking by Liz of a group photograph (overleaf), we drove the short distance to St Mary's Church, Rattery, where Paul Rose celebrated Holy Communion. David Winnington-Ingram read from Acts and Judith Rose read the Gospel. Then we set off for Plymouth. Devon lanes are narrow and we soon encountered a bus that, for some reason, was immobilised and completely blocked our way. We waited for the problem to be resolved, but time was marching towards ferry departure hour. Eventually and with much difficulty, I backed the minibus down a steep driveway and, amidst a strong smell of distressed clutch, persuaded it to extricate itself and we arrived at Plymouth Ferry Port in good time.

The crossing to Santander was without incident and by 10am DST, we were on the road to León. As the route climbed ever more steeply up the northern aspect of the Picos, the sun shone, but the minibus laboured, the engine overheated and my concern mounted. However, nature came to my rescue. A feature of advancing years, which troubled me not at the time, but increasingly does in my 77th year, is what medics refer to as urgency of micturition. *Sotto voce*, requests for a comfort break accumulated. I had driven the route before and remembered

Compostela Pilgrims Group Photograph
Photo © Liz Owen

Penny Escombe
Midgie Brassey
David Painter
Roger Watson
The Author
Judith Rose   Elisabeth Court   Paul Rose   Richard Parkinson
Jane Watson   Marjorie Blake   Mary Morrell

that a pretty village lay not far ahead, and sure enough it did, called La Hermida. I drove into the tiny, central square and parked near an attractive looking hostelry, called Posada Campo. I entered. It was eleven o'clock in the morning, when any sensible Spaniard stops what he, and it is usually 'he', is doing and drops into the local for a cup of *solo doble* expresso coffee and a modest glass of brandy. I ordered both. As they were placed on the bar before me, the rest of the party entered. When they took the scene in, some expressed surprise.

"Don't worry," I reassured them. "This is what sensible folk do in Spain at eleven o'clock in the morning."

After a moment's hesitation, David Painter announced he would follow suit and suggested the others did likewise. Most did and we took our bounty outside and enjoyed it on the terrace in the sunshine. Break over, we reached the summit of our climb not long afterwards and coasted downwards and into the city of León.

León boasts a plethora of fine buildings, the most impressive of which, its cathedral, was, when we arrived, our first port of call. Mary and I had visited it some years previously, so we had experienced just how amazing it is. Mostly built between 1205 and 1301, it is a masterpiece of the Gothic style of the mid-13th century. Magnificent on the outside, it is when the visitor ventures within its walls that its crowning glory, stained glass windows to rival those of Chartres Cathedral, overwhelms the senses. Together with the cathedrals at Burgos, itself a World Heritage Site, and Santiago de Compostela, it lies along the Camino de Santiago, the ancient pilgrim way from Roncesvalles on the French border to Santiago. Following the final occupation of Jerusalem by Islam in the Middle Ages, an occupation that persisted until the collapse of the Ottoman Empire at the end of World War I, Santiago de Compostela was the second most important pilgrimage destination after Rome, a status it has been recovering since the mid-20th century.

The next most impressive building in León is the Hostal de San Marcos, the parador, or hotel, and former 15th century monastery, where I had booked rooms for the night. As I walked into its magnificent entrance hall, I was taken aback to be greeted by two fellow Circuit Judges, Paul Clark and Jackie Davies, married to each other and both of whom I knew well. They told me that they too were on their way to Santiago, although I did not encounter them, when we were there later in the week.

Before dinner, at the suggestion of a member of the parador staff, Paul Rose, several others, although at this distance of time, I do not recall who, and I, climbed to a private room that overlooked the chapel. From behind a glass screen, we witnessed a Roman Catholic priest celebrating Mass. We followed it and then went back downstairs, where all twelve of us enjoyed a convivial meal in splendid surroundings.

*

The road between León and Santiago de Compostela is fairly level and the minibus coped. We arrived at Hotel Rosa Rosae, where I had booked rooms. It was and, looking at the relevant booking.com website today, remains simple, clean and comfortable.[9] That evening, I drove all of us into the city, parked, and we explored, stopping for supper in a tapas bar. Most of the party had never visited Spain before, but all took to tapas like ducks to water. The following day, we split up and explored the city as we wished. I visited the Pilgrim Reception Office and confirmed the arrangements for our service of Holy Communion the next morning. The welcome I received there was warm, friendly and ecumenical. Later we gathered at the hotel and, for supper, made our way to the tapas bar we had visited the evening before. Our mood was upbeat. The following day, Sunday 15 October 2006, I drove everyone into the city and, after parking the mini-bus, we walked to the Plaça de Obradoiro, the square in front of the cathedral.

Santiago de Compostela is in Galicia, an autonomous community of Spain. A number of different languages are spoken in parts of Spain and Galicia is no exception. The local tongue in Galicia and in some areas bordering it is Galician (*Gallego*), which straddles Portuguese and Castilian. "*Plaça*" is Galician. In Castilian, it is "*plaza*".

When we arrived at about 8.30am DST, the Plaça was relatively empty, and we made our way inside the most impressive Romanesque cathedral it has ever been my privilege to visit. Dare I say, it even outshines the Romanesque magnificence of Peterborough Cathedral, itself no slouch in the field.

St Andrew's Chapel lies on the eastern side of the north transept of the cathedral. David Painter celebrated Holy Communion at the altar, with me by his side, where I read the Gospel. I found the experience bizarre, but nonetheless heartening. Here were we, historically in the eyes of Rome, members of an heretical Protestant sect, celebrating the Eucharist in one of the most revered Roman Catholic cathedrals in the world. I remain profoundly grateful to the cathedral authorities for permitting us to do so.

We finished in good time and made our way back down the nave and out into the square, which was warming beneath a cloudless sky. The Plaça de Obradoiro is a vast, rectangular, open, paved space. The west front of the cathedral, called the Obradoiro Façade, and adjoining episcopal buildings flank the eastern long side of the Plaça (overleaf).

Santiago de Compostela Cathedral, Galicia, Spain
Photo © The Author

The western side of the Plaça mainly comprises the severely classical 18th century façade of the Town Hall (*Ayuntamiento*), designed by the French architect, Charles Lemaur. Its northern end is formed by the Hostal de los Reyes Católicos. Founded as a pilgrim inn and hospital by King Ferdinand of Aragón and

Queen Isabella of Castile, the Catholic Monarchs (*los Reyes Católicos*), it is a parador today and, together with the parador in the Alhambra Complex, Granada, the most expensive in Spain. Mary and I, together with our friends Anne and Laurence Marshall, had stayed in the Hostal de los Reyes Católicos some years previously. Inside, it is magnificent, but too extravagant for our pilgrimage. It is definitely worth a stay, if you are willing to afford it.

The south end of the Plaça is formed by the College of Saint Jerome (*Colego de San Gerónimo*), a 17th century building with a 15th century gateway, witnessing a strong Romanesque influence.[10]

On that Sunday, 15 October, at 11am DST, the Plaça called to my mind the open space by the Temple in Jerusalem during the Passover Week after Jesus had arrived and before he was crucified on the first Good Friday. It was heaving with pilgrims, to the extent that walking through them in a straight line was impossible. I suggested that, in order to be well-placed in the cathedral for the Pilgrim Mass at noon, we should go back inside. The others agreed and we did.

The cathedral was not yet full and we were shown by a verger to seats in the north transept, very close to Saint Andrew's Chapel and in full view of the nave altar. By noon, the cathedral was overflowing. A young priest, robed in alb and chasuble entered and stood in front of the altar. He greeted by names, citing the places from which they hailed, all those who had walked the Camino to Santiago and had given their details, as they had been invited, to the Pilgrim Reception Office. Then, he celebrated a post-Vatican II Mass, which we followed in the translation I had prepared in our printed service booklet. Some of our party left after the final blessing, which was a pity, for that was when the incense burner (*botafumeiro*) was engaged.

In the Middle Ages, when pilgrims walked the Camino of Santiago and swept into the cathedral, they had not enjoyed the benefit of baths and showers, even in the unlikely event that there were any. They exuded an overpowering, unpleasant odour, to which incense was the counter, but not just the quantity of incense used in churches today. That would not have begun to address the problem. I quote from Wikipedia's website.

> The Santiago de Compostela Botafumeiro is one of the largest censers in the world, weighing 80 kg and measuring 1.60 m in height. It is normally on display in the library of the cathedral, but for certain important religious occasions, it is brought to the floor of the cathedral and attached to a rope hung from the pulley mechanism [and] filled with 40 kilograms (88 lb) of charcoal and incense.[11]

It is not used every Sunday, because, in the past, it has been the cause of serious accidents. The most famous occurred in 1499, when, as it swung, it became detached from the rope securing it to the pulley, flew through a transept rose window and out of the cathedral. No one was injured.[10]

Fortunately, Sunday, 15 October 2006, was regarded by the cathedral authorities as an important religious occasion. The *botafumeiro* was anchored by ropes fastened to the zenith of the dome over the crossing, At the end of the service, eight men in red habits, called *tiraboleiros* (incense carriers), undid the ropes from one of the columns supporting the dome and lowered the *botafumeiro*. Then they manipulated the ropes and pulley to swing it until it almost touched the lofty ceilings of the north and south transepts, spewing out truly epic clouds of incense the while. I, for one, shall never forget it, but those of us who witnessed it were careful not to disappoint those of our party, who had left early, by saying too much afterwards about how awe-inspiring it had been.

*

We enjoyed a quick lunch in Santiago and set out for our Sunday night's stop in the parador at Gijón. I had trouble finding it, so we arrived late, but it mattered not. We ate, slept, breakfasted and departed on our way to Santander and the *Pont-Aven* ferry. We paused at Santillana del Mar, which one of our party, Richard Parkinson, had visited and loved as a child. It is an attractive old town, full of ancient buildings that originally had grown up around a monastery that sheltered the remains of St Juliana. Santillana is an abbreviation of Santa Juliana and the monastery was a famous pilgrimage destination throughout the Middle Ages.[12]

We had an early lunch there, because we were due in Santander at 2.30pm DST, an hour before the ferry sailed. The ferry left on time and we arrived at Plymouth the next morning at 9.30am BST.

I had happily driven the whole way, which at the age of 62 was no burden, especially as the weather on our journey throughout had been cloudless, but in England the minibus was about to disabuse us of the cautious praise we had bestowed upon it before boarding the ferry in Santander. As I drove up the M5 towards Bristol, it began to rain, not gently, but biblically. A cry went up from behind me and the sight that greeted my eyes when I glanced in the driving mirror remains sharp in my memory. Midgie Brassey was sitting in the middle of the last bank of seats at the back. She was wearing a Barbour jacket, borrowed from Penny Escombe, and was cradling a Barbour broad-brimmed hat on her lap to catch the stream of water that was pouring through a split in the roof of the minibus, sprinkling her features as it fell. To her well-deserved credit, she was smiling, treating it as a joke. I have since learnt that, behind me, the pilgrims countered this misfortune with hastily concocted White Lady cocktails. We arrived back in Apethorpe mid-afternoon, where David Painter, assisted by a damp but buoyant Midgie, led a short non-sacramental service in St Leonard's Church, following which, we all bade each other farewell. I know from remarks afterwards and the gifts by the pilgrims to Mary and me of two silver cockleshell caskets, that they, like us, had had a lot of fun, which is what life should be all about.

*

The following morning, I drove the minibus to the premises of Tillson Autos Ltd in Glatton. I was asked if it had been damaged and the enquirer seemed disappointed when I said it had not. When I politely pointed out the split in the roof, it evoked no apology whatsoever. I felt sorry for the next party who hired it.

A retired farmer and old friend of mine lives in Glatton. When, a few days later, we were shooting together at Holme Fen, a few miles south of Peterborough, and I told him about the minibus, he remarked,

"Well, Boy, knowing Tillsons as I do, I'm surprised you even managed to drive it out of their yard."

*

Translation

I was not convinced that the suggestion by the retired clergy that I should consider ordination had been a call from God, but if it had been, notwithstanding my licensing as a reader in 2005, I had not yet obeyed it. I was clear that, just in case, I should respond appropriately. I thought it likely that once the Church of England hierarchy had taken a good look at me, I would be told that, good chap though I was, I was not suitable material for the cloth, but it was my responsibility to discover that.

In 2005, Bill Croft had been replaced as DDO by the Reverend Canon Julie Hutchinson. I made an appointment to see her on 12 July of that year at The Old Rectory, Stanwick, a village about halfway between Peterborough and Northampton. At our meeting, she agreed to see me regularly in order to assess whether I was suitable to be ordained. From the following April we met monthly, when she gently cross-examined me about every aspect of my life, beginning with my childhood. In the process, I revealed to Julie things I have never even disclosed to Mary, let alone to anyone else, whether before or since. Her investigation of me was thorough, as it should be.

Julie decided that I might fit the bill, so it was arranged that, together with other candidates from around the Midlands, I would attend a three-day residential assessment between Monday and Wednesday, 3 to 5 July 2006, by the Bishops' Advisory Panel at a location in the West Midlands. The day I left for it, I received a text message of warm support from Ian Cundy, the then Bishop of Peterborough, whom, as a judge, I had previously met several times at gatherings of Northamptonshire's great and good.

Despite my scepticism as to whether my character and temperament qualified me for the priesthood, to my surprise I was accepted for ordination training and Ian Cundy kindly decided that I needed to undergo only two years of theological instruction, instead of the usual three.

Needless to say, I was delighted and shared the good news with Mary. She told me she was pleased for me. Then she added,

"But, you know, darling, there's something that worries me about you."

"What's that?"

"Well," she replied with a smile, "in both the professions you have chosen to follow, you have to wear a frock."

My theological training course began in September 2006, two weeks before I led the pilgrimage to Santiago de Compostela. When I had completed the course nearly two years later, the Reverend Canon Stephen Evans, then Rector of Uppingham, Rutland, agreed to accept me as his curate. So it was that, on 6 July 2008, in the presence of Mary, Stephen Evans and other friends and relatives, I was ordained deacon, together with several others, in Peterborough Cathedral.

I had obeyed God's call.

*

As will be apparent, Midgie Brassey, maybe unwittingly had played a seminal role in my journey to ordination. I should have welcomed the opportunity of sharing what I have written here with her, but, sadly, that is not possible. Much mourned by her many friends, including, it goes without saying, Mary and me, Midgie died on 27 August, 2019. *Requiescat in pace.*

*

Curate

I count myself extremely lucky that, when I embarked upon the three professions I have chosen to follow, solicitor, barrister and Anglican priest, I have enjoyed the inestimable advantage in each of an outstanding mentor.

Instead of founding his eponymous firm in Peterborough in the 1930s, Charles Greenwood could have practised in the City of London and become a national leader of his profession. As it was, he was a born and bred East Anglian and preferred to practise in the City of Peterborough, where, by common consent, he was one of the best solicitors, whose services were sought after from a wide surrounding area. When, for thirty months between 1967 and 1969, I was being trained by him hands-on as his articled clerk, he taught me much that has stood me in good stead ever since. One lesson I have drawn upon time and time again is that, when faced with a decision in a complex negotiation or difficult dispute and the course to adopt is unclear, his advice was: Do nothing. Let the other side make a mistake and then capitalise on it.

As I have described earlier, in 1974 I left Greenwoods and was called to the Bar. I then spent six months as the pupil of Igor Judge. Igor taught me how to write succinct and unpretentious English prose and to be bold. One day, when I had drafted a written advice about some obtuse legal dilemma, pointing out the difficulties in the case and that the outcome was uncertain, Igor rebuked me.

"Peter, the client is not paying you to tell him what the problems are. He's paying you for your opinion as to how to solve them."

On another occasion,

"Peter, the only thing that matters in the Law is to be right."

Excellent advice that, like Charles Greenwood's, has stood me in good stead professionally.

The third outstanding mentor was my training incumbent at Uppingham. Stephen Evans was 47 when I joined him in July 2008. I was 64 and an experienced and serving Circuit Judge, accustomed to exercising authority. Stephen never said so, but being landed with me as a trainee must have been a challenge for him. Fortunately, Stephen is a strong character, who, I quickly judged, would stand no nonsense. Shortly after I joined him, we fell out following a marriage rehearsal with a prospective bride and groom. The details of our disagreement matter not, but it taught me that I would learn little if I argued with him and that he had much to teach me. I took care not fall out with him again and he certainly did. I remain deeply grateful to him for the trouble he took with me.

One example of his good advice concerned sermons. My theological training for ordination had been delivered by the Eastern Region Ministry Course,[13] then affiliated to the Anglia Ruskin University, Cambridge. It had been attended by both Anglican and Methodist ordinands and the standard of training was theologically, rather than practically, sound. A notable omission from the course was instruction on preaching. Preaching is a hugely important component of most worship services, but my experience of sermons, whenever I sit in the pew, which is not often these days, but used to be frequent, is that quality is variable. One difference between a cleric and a barrister is that the cleric's future prosperity does not depend upon skill in the pulpit. On the other hand, a poor performance by a barrister in court in a provincial town is quickly broadcast amongst local solicitors and the barrister will be lucky to receive another brief from any law firm in that town.

Not only does a barrister have to learn to be proficient and persuasive before a jury, he or she has also to be the same before a single judge, or, a greater challenge, a bank of three Lord and

Lady Justices in the Court of Appeal. My practice at the Bar had been busy and I had learnt how to speak effectively in public. I needed no tuition in that regard, but some of my fellow ordinands certainly would have benefitted from it, had it been on offer, which it was not.

Once I had become licensed as a reader, I had preached regularly in Apethorpe Church and sometimes in other churches, so I thought I knew how to do it. I appreciated the danger of losing the attention of my listeners and adopted a personal rule that my sermons would not exceed 1,200 words, which take about eleven minutes to deliver.

The first sermon I preached at Uppingham was on Sunday, 27 July 2008. When Stephen asked me to do so, he added:

"But I'm not going to allow you to preach to my people, unless I first approve it. Okay?"

I returned to New Sulehay and crafted an offering based upon two passages from Matthew, Chapter 13, the Gospel reading set for the following Sunday, in which Jesus recounts the Parable of the Weeds to the crowd and afterwards explains its meaning to his disciples.

When I had completed my 1,200 or so words, I emailed it to Stephen. Later that week, when we met in Uppingham Rectory, Stephen said to me,

"I've read your sermon, Peter."

"Is it all right, Stephen?"

"The content's fine, but if you go on that long, my people will start throwing hymn books at you."

"Oh!" I was both surprised and disappointed. "So, how long should it be then?"

"No more than 900 words."

Some years ago in the USA, research was conducted into the appropriate length of an advocate's speech to a jury. In a real trial, but using a parallel jury of twelve people, the academics discovered that three stopped listening after three minutes and all twelve after ten. Competent barristers are aware of the risk of losing an audience, so they employ devices, such as inviting jurors to look at a photograph, or a diagram, or a copy document, in order to maintain their attention, but a preacher is constrained as to what can be done from the pulpit.

A sermon of 900 words preached by me takes between seven and a half and eight minutes to deliver, which pretty much guarantees the engagement from beginning to end of all but the most uninterested listener. Since Stephen Evans gave me that advice, no sermon I have preached at a service of Holy Communion has exceeded 900 words, as anyone will verify who has looked at the published collection of my sermons, *From the Pulpit, Home and Abroad*. The only exceptions to this rule have been sermons I have occasionally preached at Book of Common Prayer Evensong, when a slightly longer offering is expected.

*

Apart from saying a prayer from the bench, robed in a cassock, surplice and black preaching scarf, on every Remembrance Day when the courts were sitting, there has been only one occasion when my calling as an Anglican minister intersected with my duties as a judge. A little background is necessary.

The Crown Courts in England deal with serious criminal cases. When such cases are called on for the first time, the defendant, after he or she has been identified, is asked whether he or she pleads 'guilty' or 'not guilty'. If the plea is 'not guilty', the case is adjourned for trial by jury and directions are given by the judge concerning witnesses, exhibits, estimated length of trial and venue. On the other hand, if the defendant pleads 'guilty', the case is adjourned for sentence, usually to a date

Stephen continued,

"And, Peter?"

"Yes, Stephen?"

"I want you to pronounce the Latin as they do now in the Vatican and not in the bowdlerised version you used at Westminster School. Understood?"

"Yes, Stephen. Understood."

"If you go online, there is a site that sets out how Ecclesiastical Latin is pronounced. I recommend you take a look at it."

"Thank you, Stephen. I shall."

I did. Searching online as I write this, there are a number of websites that advise how Ecclesiastical Latin is pronounced in the Roman Catholic Church. Ten years ago, I downloaded from one of them and the detailed result, comprising three pages, is stored in my laptop. A website today summarises the position more succinctly.

> Ecclesiastical or Church Latin follows essentially the same spelling and pronunciation rules as those of modern Italian, with some minor variations; e.g. consonants are never held. (Classical Latin has its own rules.) This is the pronunciation used when singing Ecclesiastical Latin.[15]

Armed with the text of the service, I set to, rehearsing in my study at home the pronunciation of those parts of the liturgy that, as celebrant, I was going to perform; and performing is how I viewed it; and how it turned out on the day. A copy of the liturgy we used is at **Appendix B**. The original was in a larger font. The pieces that the celebrant says are printed in light black, the responses to be spoken by the congregation in bold black, and the choral parts in red.

*

Another digression is necessary in order to explain what happened on the night when I led the service in what I intended would be impeccably pronounced modern Ecclesiastical Latin.

From 1977 until 1996, Mary and I owned a delightful cottage on the banks of the River Conon in Ross-shire, a river in which we fished for wild salmon every spring. When we sold the cottage, my family decided we should buy another holiday home somewhere with a better and more reliable climate than the Scottish Highlands and within inexpensive reach of New Sulehay. I had left Oxford not only with a degree in French, but also with fluency in that tongue, which I had to have to gain my degree; and I was also fluent in German, as I explain at page 74.

My instinct as a linguist militated against presenting myself abroad as the archetypical Brit, who, ignorant of the language spoken where he or she finds him- or herself, compensates by speaking English very loudly in the vain belief that he or she will be understood. It followed that the obvious choice of a nearby country that enjoyed good weather was France. However, the plan was to spend every spring and autumn in our projected holiday home so as to extend the summer climate that prevails here in England. In 1997, property in Provence was expensive and in Gascony, situated as it is in the shadow of the Pyrenees where houses were cheaper, spring and autumn can be cool. In those days, our good friends, Anne and Laurence Marshall, whom I have already mentioned, owned a delightful second home overlooking the Mediterranean in the Costa Blanca, about three miles south of Jávea, Spain. In the late 1990s, we had stayed with them in February and were much taken with both the country and the weather. So, we decided to investigate buying a house in that part of Spain. In February 1997, after an extensive search of particulars supplied by an English estate agent, who specialised in marketing holiday homes in Spain, and a trip by our daughter, Harriet, to inspect likely properties, we bought a house in Alcalalí, a village some ten miles inland from Jávea in the Marina Alta, a range of low limestone mountains that stretches from mainland Spain under the Mediterranean to Majorca.

I then spoke very little Spanish, or, more correctly Castilian, and was determined to repair my deficiency. Between 1997 and 2001, I took lessons twice weekly with Spanish *assistantes* at nearby Oundle School and today, although not fluent, I can converse in reasonably competent Castilian. An important feature of classical Castilian is pronunciation. As anyone who speaks it will know, consonants are articulated differently than in English. By way of two examples, 'c' is not a sibilant, but is pronounced 'th' and 'v' is pronounced 'b', and there are other idiosyncratic features of spoken Castilian. Although I app-roached learning to speak it conscientiously, by the autumn of 2009, when I led the All Souls service in Ecclesiastical Latin in the Church of Saints Peter and Paul, Uppingham, I was still on a learning curve.

*

All Souls Day 2009 and Uppingham Church was full. The event was being held in aid of charity and when I emerged from the vestry, robed in traditional Catholic fashion, I thought, 'So far, so good'. The choir was magnificent and, as I led worship in word-perfect Latin, in my estimation my pronunciation was faultless.

As history so often teaches, *nemesis* treads upon the heels of *hubris*. When, by the North Porch, I was bidding farewell to members of the congregation, several remarked that they had been unsure whether I had been speaking Ecclesiastical Latin or modern Spanish. My assiduity in learning how to pronounce Castilian correctly had subconsciously influenced my rendering

of Ecclesiastical Latin. A smidgeon of disappointment, tinged
with rueful amusement, lingers to this day.

Ss Peter & Paul Church, Uppingham, Rutland
Photo © The Author

*

In July 2010, Stephen Evans left Uppingham to take up the
prestigious post of Rector of St Marylebone in London, which,
with still a year to serve of my three-year curacy, left me
without a training incumbent. I was asked by Peterborough
Diocese, and agreed, to return to my home parish of Nassington
and serve the remainder of my curacy under its then splendid
priest-in-charge, Bishop John Flack.

I led worship and preached for the last time in Saints Peter
and Paul Church, Uppingham on 26 September 2010. The
occasion was Harvest Festival and, as happened then in
Uppingham Church once a month, it was an All-Age service,

with the focus on children. The usual Sunday morning congreg-ation for Holy Communion according to Common Worship numbered about 120. The same number of adults attended an All-Age service, but on this occasion augmented by some 20 youngsters. The atmosphere was relaxed and, in place of a formal sermon, I conducted an interactive dialogue with the children, aided by a huge screen and a PowerPoint display of various aspects of farming, encompassing autumn drilling through winter and spring to harvest at the end of summer. Children and adults engaged enthusiastically, which pleased me greatly. At the end, I looked over the children at the adults sitting behind them and said,

I conclude by thanking you all for the generosity with which you have welcomed me into what Father Stephen calls your Household of God; and by wishing you well. The principle that has guided me throughout my life is, 'If it ain't fun, it ain't worth doing'. My time amongst you in Uppingham has been great fun and well worth doing. I shall treasure the memory of it and keep you all in my prayers.

*

Home

St Mary & All Saints Church, Nassington, Northamptonshire
Photo © The Author

On the first four Sundays of October 2010, following my departure from Uppingham, I attended, successively, a Justice Service for the judiciary at St Mary's Church, Cambridge, a Quiet Day at Launde Abbey, Leicestershire, Holy Communion at St Marylebone Church, led by Stephen Evans, and Parish Communion at St Andrew's Church, Much Hadham, Hertford-shire, on a weekend that Mary and I were spending with our daughter, Harriet and her husband, Charlie, nearby in Stocking Pelham, which is where they were then living.

Acting as Bishop John's deacon, in lay terms his assistant, it was on the fifth Sunday in October, the 31st and Festival of All Saints, that I attended my first service as a curate in St Mary & All Saints, Nassington.

In 2010, Nassington Benefice comprised four parishes. As well as Nassington, they were Yarwell, Woodnewton and Apethorpe and I first led worship as a priest in the benefice in Woodnewton on Sunday 7 November 2010, when I preached on Luke, Chapter 20, verses 27 to 38.

Since then, I have pursued my ministry both locally and in the Costa Blanca Chaplaincy in Spain, leading worship, cond-ucting baptisms, marriages and funerals. It has proved person-ally rewarding, even if, for the most part, it has been routine.

Bishop John Flack, with whom I became friendly, celebrated his final service in Nassington on 30 September 2012. He was followed by the Reverend Michael Matthews, who was induct-ed, or instituted, the terms are effectively interchangeable, on 28 July 2013. During his incumbency, the Nassington Benefice was reformulated to embrace, in addition to the four parishes already mentioned, the parish of Thornhaugh-cum-Wansford, with its two churches, and renamed the Watersmete Benefice.

Michael Matthews departed on 10 October 2015 and, on 24 September 2016, he was succeeded by The Reverend Jane Tailby, who remains the incumbent today and with whom I relate and work well.

Giles Machin died suddenly on 17 December 2016 and a day or so later, John Machin telephoned me and asked me if I would preside over Giles' funeral and memorial services, fixed for Tuesday 10 January 2017. I was very sad, but honoured to be invited and agreed to do so. So it was that, on 4 January 2017, I drove once again up the A1 Great North Road to Normanton On Trent to plan both services.

Giles Machin
Photo © Machin family

Giles and Sharon's home was in the village of Eaton in Nottinghamshire. There was to be a small family funeral in All Saints, Eaton parish church, at 10.30am, followed by a light lunch at Sharon's house. The memorial service was to be held in St Swithun's Church, Retford. John, Sue and I settled the content of both services, the former to be shared with the non-ordained incumbent at Eaton, Angela Morfett-Jones, and the latter to be conducted by me alone.

As I left, John said to me,

"Lottie and Mike have left a present for you."

He indicated a parcel on the hall table.

I unwrapped it to discover leather-bound editions of my three Pepynbridge novels, in the first of which was written,

> *Dear Peter,*
> *Thank you for presiding so beautifully over our wedding.*
> *Best wishes,*
> *Charlotte and Mike*

Unexpected endorsement is always a joy to receive, and not just a joy, but encouraging as well. Leaders of worship and judges never sit in the body of a church or court to witness their own performance.

*

The weather on 10 January was mercifully fine and mild. Dona Machin had been Welsh and at All Saints Church, after I had smoothed the ruffled feathers of Angela Morfett-Jones, who understandably betrayed some resentment at sharing the leadership of the service with me, we concluded the brief funeral in the morning with a hearty rendition of *Cwm Rhondda*. After the pallbearers had lowered Giles into a grave in the churchyard, the members of his family, together with Mary and me, covered the couple of hundred yards to Sharon's house.

Whenever I conduct a funeral or memorial service at which someone else is to deliver the eulogy, I ask to see it in advance. It is the duty of the minister leading either service to give an address with some theological content, but, when doing so, it is important not to trespass upon another's eulogy. There was neither an address, nor a eulogy, at the short funeral service at Eaton, but at the memorial service, where I would be giving an address, the eulogy was to be delivered by Nigel Bruce, a friend of Giles from his schooldays at Ruthin.

A few days before the service, Nigel emailed me his eulogy. It was long, but comprehensive and engaging and did justice to Giles. It was not my place to criticise it, even if I had thought it right to do so, which I did not.

At Sharon's, I confined myself to one sausage and one small glass of wine. As I sipped it, a big chap, over six feet tall and built like a second-row rugby union forward, approached me.

"Peter?"

His manner and tone were diffident, self-deprecating.

"Yes."

"Peter, I'm Nigel Bruce."

"Ah, the eulogy!"

"Yes. Is it all right?"

"Nigel, it's excellent. It's longer than usual, but given what you have to say about Giles, there's nothing wrong with that."

"Oh, good."

He both sounded and looked relieved. Then he frowned.

"Peter, there's something that worries me."

"What's that, Nigel?"

"Well, I've never done anything quite like this before and I'm pretty nervous."

"You'll be all right Nigel. Don't worry about it."

"Oh, but I do."

He paused for what seemed like an age, whilst I waited patiently, my head slightly tilted and wearing what I hoped was an anxiously helpful expression. Then he asked,

"Peter, what should I do, if I ..." He stumbled.

"If you do what?"

He gazed at me, too diffident to articulate his concern. I decided to help him.

"Do you mean, if you dry?"

His face betrayed profound relief.

"Yes, Peter, that is what I mean. Does it happen to you?"

"Can do, but you know what I do when I sense it coming on?"

"No, what?"

"I clench my buttocks," I replied truthfully.

"You what?"

His tone and expression were incredulous. I smiled encouragingly.

"I clench my buttocks, really, really hard."

"Does it work?"

"It does for me. Try it. And good luck!"

"Thank you."

St Swithun's Church, Retford, is huge, cathedral-like. It was a measure of how widely known and respected Giles was in Nottinghamshire and farther afield that, when I walked in at about a quarter to three, the church was packed. It was estimated afterwards that there had been about 300 people there, but there could well have been more.

After the Introduction and Collect, *Cwm Rhondda* was sung with gusto. The congregation was in celebratory mood, sad no doubt at losing a dear brother and friend, but resolved to send him off heartily, as he deserved. Following a passage from Revelation, read by John Machin, I gave my address, the opening of which is at pages 243-244. Next, *Dear Lord and Father of Mankind* rang out across Retford Town, and then, maintaining the Welsh flavour of the service, from an elevated ambo, just across from where I was sitting in the chancel, Giles's son, William, read, *Do not go gentle into that good night*, by Dylan Thomas.

St Swithun's Church, Retford, Nottinghamshire
Photo © Julian P Guffogg (cc-by-sa/2.0)

William was followed into the ambo by Nigel Bruce. He started well enough, but, after a few minutes, he faltered. He cleared his throat and tried again, but in vain. No sound emerged. He looked up despairingly from his script at the assembled company, took a deep breath and, gesturing across the chancel towards me, said,

"You know what Peter told me to do if this happened? He told me to clench my buttocks."

There was a moment's pause before the laughter began, hesitatingly at first, but then swelling to fill the church. Nigel looked relieved and, when quiet resumed, he continued. Twice more during his delivery, he paused. His listeners, he knew, were with him now, in the palm of his hand and, playing them, he again looked over the top of his spectacles to announce,

"Another buttock-clenching moment."

More laughter. It made the service, which concluded with a deafening rendition of *Jerusalem*.

Three days later, on Saturday, 13 January 2017, I received the following letter from John Machin.

> *Dear Peter,*   *12.i.17*
>
> *I can't tell you how thankful we are to you for all you did in connection with dear old Giles. You made the grief so much more bearable and so skilfully moved us from mourning (the funeral) to celebration (the memorial service).*
>
> *We have been so blessed to have a good, old, generous friend who has supported us this last year in both happy and sad(?) times and I can't begin to tell you how much you have meant to us all and how much we appreciate the time and trouble you took over the arrangements – not least to navigate the lively waters surrounding the minister i/c Eaton!*
>
> *It was lovely seeing Mary and I hope we'll meet very soon in less buttock clenching circumstances!*
>
> *With much gratitude and every best wish to you both from Sue and me,*
>
> *Yours ever,*
>
> *John*

A minister of religion couldn't ask for more than that!

*

During my ministry as layman, reader, deacon and priest, I have taken many services for different purposes, but none beats the memorial service I led in honour of Giles Machin in St

Swithun's Church, Retford, on 10 January 2017. I opened *Collared* with the question *Why?* Amongst all the liturgical performances I have given, so far as I am concerned, the memorial service for Giles Machin best answers that question.

As Jesus once said to his disciples, James and John, and quoted at the beginning of this book,

> Among you, whoever wants to be great must be your servant
> and whoever wants to be first must be the willing slave of all.[16]

Thank you for reading these reminiscences. I hope you have enjoyed them as much as I enjoyed living them.

May God be with you!

***

agus. It thereby acquired the status of a relic and doubtless enabled its possessor to recoup the cost of his pilgrimage from credulous friends and acquaintances on his return home.

The heyday of this cult was from the 12th to the 15th century. It was fostered by kings, popes and bishops and flourished on the concept of James as the powerful defender of Christendom against Islam, testified to by many miracle stories of varying antiquity and credibility. To this day, St James or Santiago, Matamoros, Slayer of the Moors, is the patron saint of Spain.

The mediaeval tradition of pilgrimage began to decline as the influence of the Reformation spread across Northern Europe. Sir Francis Drake declared that Compostela was "the ultimate hotbed of papish superstition" and vowed to repeat the deed of Al Mansur. Fortunately, the intrepid and swashbuckling adventurer and favourite of Queen Elizabeth never succeeded, although, in 1589, he raided the nearby port city of La Coruña.

Work carried out on the high altar in the 17th century damaged the vault of the old burial chamber and the precise whereabouts of the relics thereafter remained a mystery until 1878. In that year, the Archbishop of Santiago set out to find the Apostle's remains and, at the same time, to modify the high altar and display the relics for veneration by the faithful. In January 1878, a hole was dug into the old burial vault and an urn containing the skeletons of three men was found. The Vatican then conducted extensive investigations and, on the 19th July 1884, the bones were declared to be the remains of the Apostle and his two disciples. No rigorous academic, let alone an Anglican sceptical of all things Roman, would be satisfied that such a pronouncement was conclusive of the truth. However, there has been a further twist to the tale.

The contents of the urn were placed in a casket in full view beneath the high altar and the vault, which in fact contains three tombs, was resealed. In September 1988, a professor named Millan from the Institute of Theological Studies in Santiago visited the tombs. He noticed that in one and only one of them, there is a pilgrims' hole, a 'fenestella confessionis'. He inserted an endoscope and photographed the interior. Fascinatingly, this revealed the presence of an inscription that read 'Athanasius Martyr'. Athanasius was traditionally one of those whose remains accompanied those of St James from Jerusalem to Spain in the first century. The inscription was, as one would expect, in Greek save for two letters, one of which was Semitic and the other Aramaic. In the opinion of some historians, this strongly suggests that the tomb was constructed, not in Spain, but in Palestine, and provides strong support for the hypothesis that the remains in the casket are indeed those of St James the Great, St Athanasius and St Theodore.

This is all fascinating stuff, but does it matter? I think it does, because so much of religion is about symbols and Christianity is no exception. The symbol of the crucifix reminds of the central truth of our faith every time we behold it. The fact that it is not the actual cross upon which our Lord was crucified is neither here nor there. Santiago de Compostela is a symbol of martyrdom, of St James' loyalty to Jesus and his mission, an example of a person who put truth first in his life and of his mission to spread the Gospel at whatever cost to himself. In the end, it cost him his earthly life but has brought him immortality. All that he symbolised lives on in that casket beneath the high altar in Santiago de Compostela.

In recent times, Santiago de Compostela has once again become a centre of pilgrimage. Thousands make their way there every year, particularly at this time. Some fly. Some drive. But many walk the Camino de Santiago from the French border across the breadth of Northern Spain to Compostela. Last year, a local man cycled from Inverness to Santiago de Compostela to raise money for charity. I know because I was one of many who sponsored him. So that great cathedral housing the supposed remains of St James is now the inspiration for the raising of money for the physically needy and for the renewing of the faith of the spiritually hungry.

Thus does St James, son of Zebedee, brother of John and trusted intimate of Jesus, continue to fulfil the charge given to Simon Peter and arguably, because he was present, to him as well by his risen Master on the shore of Lake Tiberius, "Feed my sheep". His martyrdom was not in vain.

Appendix B

THE GREETING

+ In nomine Patris, et Filii, et Spiritus Sancti.
All **Amen.**

CHOIR: INTROIT AND KYRIE
Requiem aeternam dona eis Domine, et lux perpetua luceat eis. Te
decet hymnus Deus in Sion, et tibi reddetur votum in Jerusalem.
Exaudi orationem meam, ad te omnis caro veniet.
Kyrie eleison, Christe eleison, Kyrie eleison.

THE COLLECT

Dominus vobiscum.
All **Et cum spiritu tuo.**

Oremus.

Fidelium Deus, omnium conditor et redemptory, animabus
famulorum famularumque tuarum remissionem cunctorum tribue
peccatorum; ut indulgentiam quam semper optaverunt, piis
supplicationibus consequantur per Jesum Christum Dominum
nostrum, per quem et cum quo, in unitate Sancti Spiritus, sit tibi,
omnipotens Pater, omnis honor et gloria, in omnem æternitatem.
All **Amen.**

Please sit.

THE LITURGY OF THE WORD

A READING

When the Epistle is announced the reader says

A reading from the Epistle of Paul to the Corinthians

1 Corinthians 15. 51-57

At the end of the reading the reader says

This is the word of the Lord.
All **Thanks be to God.**

HYMN

THE GRADUAL AND TRACT

Words from Psalm 23.

Please stand.

THE GOSPEL READING

John 6.51-55

When the gospel is announced the reader says,

+ Hear the gospel of our Lord Jesus Christ according to John.
All **Glory to you, O Lord.**

At the end,

This is the gospel of the Lord.
All **Praise to you, O Christ.**

Words from Psalm 42

Please remain standing.

THE LITURGY OF THE SACRAMENT

THE PEACE

Pax Domini sit semper vobiscum.
All **Et cum spiritu tuo.**

THE PREPARATION OF THE TABLE
THE TAKING OF THE BREAD AND WINE

The table is prepared.
Bread and wine are placed upon it.

Please sit.

CHOIR: THE OFFERTORY
O Domine Jesu Christe, Rex gloriae, libera animas defunctorum de poenis inferni, et de profundo lacu, libera eas de ore leonis, ne absorbeat eas tartarus, ne cadant in obscurum. Hostias et preces tibi Domine laudis offerimus, tu suscipe pro animabus illis, quarum hodie memoriam facimus; fac eas, Domine, de morte transire ad vitam. Quam olim Abrahae promisisti et semini ejus.

THE EUCHARISTIC PRAYER

Please stand.

Dominus vobiscum.
All **Et cum spiritu tuo.**

Sursum corda.
All **Habemus ad Dominum.**

Gratias agamus Domino Deo nostro.
All **Dignum et justum est.**

Vere dignum et justum est, æquum et salutare, nos tibi semper et ubique gratias agere, Domine Sancte, Pater Omnipotens, æterne Deus.

Memento etiam, Domine, famulorum famularumque tuarum qui nos praecesserunt cum signo fidei, et dormiunt in somno pacis. Ipsis, Domine, et omnibus in Christo quiescentibus, locum refrigerii, lucis et pacis, ut indulgeas, deprecamur.

Ideo cum Angelis et Archangelis, cum Thronis et Dominationibus, cumque omni militia cœlestis exercitus, hymnum gloriæ tuæ canimus, sine fine dicentes,

CHOIR:
Sanctus, Sanctus, Sanctus, Dominus Deus Sabaoth. Pleni sunt caeli et terra gloria tua. Hosanna in excelsis.

O Deus omnipotens, Pater noster cœlestis, qui ex immensa tua misericordia dedisti nobis unicum Filium tuum Jesum Christum, pro nostra redemptione mortem in cruce pati, ibique unica illa oblatione qua sese semel obtulit, perfectum, plenum, et sufficiens sacrificium, hostiam et satisfactionem integram faceret pro peccatis totius mundi, quique instituit, ac in suo Sacrosancto Evangelio præcepit perpetuam memoriam preciosæ suæ mortis celebrare, usque dum rediret.

Exaudi nos quæsumus, misericors Pater, et concede, ut nos sumentes has creaturas Panis et Vini, juxta sacrosanctam institutionem Filii tui, Salvatoris nostri Jesu Christi, in memoriam ejus diræ mortis et passionis, participes simus sanctissimi Corporis et Sanguinis ejus.

Qui eadem nocte qua tradebatur, accepit Panem, et + gratias agens fregit, ac dedit discipulis suis, dicens, Accipite, comedite, hoc est Corpus meum, quod pro vobis datur, hoc facite in meam commemorationem.

Simili modo, postquam cœnatum est, accepit Calicem, et + gratias agens dedit illis, dicens, Bibite ex eo omnes, hic est enim Sanguis meus novi Testamenti, qui pro vobis et pro multis effunditur, in remissionem peccatorum, hoc facite, quotiescunque biberitis, in meam commemorationem.

O Domine cœlestis Pater, nos humiles servi tui supplices rogamus paternam bonitatem, ut hoc nostrum sacrificium laudis et gratiarum actionis, benigne accipias, humiliter supplicantes, ut propter merita et mortem Filii tui Jesu Christi, et per fidem in illius sanguinem, concedas, ut nos cum universa Ecclesia remissionem peccatorum ceteraque beneficia passionis illius consequamur.

Atque hic etiam offerimus, et præsentamus tibi, Domine, nos ipsos, animas nostras, et corpora nostra, hostiam rationalem, sanctam, et vivam, humiliter obsecrantes, ut quotquot participes sumus hujus Sacrosanctæ Communionis, tua gratia et cœlesti benedictione repleamur.

Et quanquam indigni sumus, propter multitudinem peccatorem nostrorum, qui tibi ullam sacrificium offeramus, tamen supplicamus, ut acceptam habeas hanc nostram servitutem, non intuendo nostra merita, sed condonando nostra peccata, + per Jesum Christum Dominum nostrum, per quem et cum quo, in unitate Sancti Spiritus, sit tibi, omnipotens Pater, omnis honor et gloria, in omnem æternitatem.
All **Amen.**

CHOIR:
Pie Jesu Domine, dona eis requiem, dona eis sempiternam requiem.

THE LORD'S PRAYER

Oremus

Praeceptis salutaribus moniti, et divina institutione formati, audemus dicere,

CHOIR:
Pater noster, qui es in coelis, sanctificetur nomen tuum, adveniat regnum tuum, fiat voluntas tua, sicut in coelo, et in terra. Panem nostrum quotidianum da nobis hodie, et dimitte nobis debita nostra, sicut et nos dimittimus debitoribus nostris. Et ne nos inducas in tentationem. Sed libera nos a malo. Amen.

THE BREAKING OF THE BREAD

The president breaks the consecrated bread during the singing of the Agnus Dei.

CHOIR: THE AGNUS DEI

Agnus Dei, qui tollis peccata mundi, dona eis requiem.
Agnus Dei, qui tollis peccata mundi, dona eis requiem.
Agnus Dei, qui tollis peccata mundi, dona eis sempiternam requiem.
Lux aeterna luceat eis Domine, cum sanctis tuis in aeternum, quia pius es.
Requiem aeternam dona eis Domine; et lux perpetua luceat eis.

THE GIVING OF COMMUNION

The president invites people to receive Holy Communion.

Ecce Agnus Dei, ecce qui tollit peccata mundi.
All **Domine, non sum dignus, ut intres sub tectum meum: sed tantum dic verbo, et sanabitur anima mea.**

The Choir and the people receive Communion.

Corpus Domini nostri Jesu Christi

Sanguis Domini nostri Jesu Christi

CHOIR ANTHEM: During the Communion the choir sings Cantique de Jean Racine.

Verbe, égal au Très Haut, notre unique espérance, jour éternel de la terre et des cieux; de la paisible nuit nous rompons le silence, Divin Sauveur, jette sur nous les yeux! Répands sur nous le feu de ta grâce puissante, que tout l'enfer fuie au son de ta voix; dissipe le sommeil d'une âme languissante, qui la conduit à l'oubli de tes lois! O Christ, sois favorable à ce peuple fidèle pour te bénir maintenant rassemblé. Reçois les chants qu'il offre à ta gloire immortelle, et de tes dons qu'il retourne comblé!

THE POSTCOMMUNION

PRAYER AFTER COMMUNION

The president says the post communion prayer.

Dominus vobiscum.
All **Et cum spiritu tuo.**

Oremus.
Animabus quæsumus, Domine, famulorum famularumque tuarum
oratio proficiat supplicantium, ut eas et a peccatis omnibus exuas, et
tuæ redemptionis facias esse participes per Jesum Christum
Dominum nostrum, per quem et cum quo, in unitate Sancti Spiritus,
sit tibi, omnipotens Pater, omnis honor et gloria, in omnem
æternitatem.
All **Amen.**

CHOIR:
Libera me, Domine, de morte aeterna, in die illa tremenda, quando
coeli movendi sunt et terra, dum veneris judicare saeculum per
ignem. Tremens factus sum ego, et timeo, dum discussio venerit,
atque ventura ira. Dies illa, dies irae, calamitatis et miseriae, dies
magna et amara valde. Requiem aeternam dona eis, Domine, et lux
perpetua luceat eis.

THE DISMISSAL

Dominus vobiscum.
All **Et cum spiritu tuo.**

Pax Dei, quæ superat omnem intellectum, conservet corda vestra et
mentes vestras, in cogitatione, et amore Dei, et Filii ejus Jesu Christi
Domini nostril, et + favor omnipotentis Dei, Patris, Filii, et Spiritus
Sancti, vobis adsit, semperque vobiscum maneat.
All **Amen.**

Deac. Ite, Missa est.
All **Deo gratias.**

CHOIR: THE ANTIPHON
In Paradisum deducant te angeli, in tuo adventu suscipiant te
martyres, et perducant te in civitatem sanctam Jerusalem. Chorus

angelorum te suscipiat, et cum Lazaro quondam paupere aeternam habeas requiem.

The congregation is invited to leave in silence.

***

NOTES

Wandervogel

1. https://www.wine-searcher.com/find/schloss+johannisberg+tba+rheingau+Germany (accessed 061119)
2. https://www.laywheeler.com/product-detail?id=22170662 (accessed 061119)
3. https://lincolnwhiskyshop.co.uk/ (accessed 061119)
4. https://en.wikipedia.org/wiki/Heilbronn#1900%E2%80%931945 (accessed 071119)
5. https://www.kloster-maulbronn.de/en/monastery/ (accessed 071119)
6. https://en.wikipedia.org/wiki/Pforzheim#World_War_II (accessed 071119)
7. https://en.wikipedia.org/wiki/Black_Forest (accessed 190421)
8. https://modernlanguages.sas.ac.uk/library/germanic-archives/hf-garten-papers (accessed 040520)
9. https://en.wikipedia.org/wiki/Erasmus#Death (accessed 290520)
10. https://en.wikipedia.org/wiki/St_Martin%27s_Chapel (accessed 281220)

Hustings

1. https://en.wikipedia.org/wiki/Paul_de_Lamerie (accessed 280420)
2. https://en.wikipedia.org/wiki/Marquess_of_Exeter (accessed 040520)
3. https://www.burghley.co.uk/about-burghley/family-now/ (accessed 040520)
4. Moore, C. *Margaret Thatcher, The Authorised Biography*. Volume One. 2013. London. Allen Lane. p243.
5. https://en.wikipedia.org/wiki/Raymond_Fletcher (accessed 300420)
6. https://www.britannica.com/technology/Concorde (accessed 300420)
7. https://en.wikipedia.org/wiki/Abraham_Flint (accessed 300420)
8. https://en.wikipedia.org/wiki/Stephen_Gethins (accessed 300420)
9. https://en.wikipedia.org/wiki/10_Rillington_Place (accessed 010121)
10. https://en.wikipedia.org/wiki/Peter_Rost_(politician) (accessed 040520)
11. https://en.wikipedia.org/wiki/1973_oil_crisis (accessed 300420)
12. https://en.wikipedia.org/wiki/Three-Day_Week (accessed 300420)
13. https://www.globalcitizen.org/en/content/coal-mine-woodland-trust-wildlife-trees-derby/ (accessed 010520)
14. https://en.wikipedia.org/wiki/Yorkshire_Miners%27_Association (accessed 010520)
15. https://en.wikipedia.org/wiki/Selsdon_Group (accessed 010520)
16. https://en.wikipedia.org/wiki/Upper_Clyde_Shipbuilders (accessed 010520)
17. https://en.wikipedia.org/wiki/John_Brown_%26_Company (accessed 010520)
18. https://en.wikipedia.org/wiki/Anthony_Barber (accessed 010520)
19. https://en.wikipedia.org/wiki/Ilkeston_(UK_Parliament_constituency) (accessed 010520)

Scribbling

1. https://www.lexico.com/definition/political (accessed 020520)
2. https://en.wikipedia.org/wiki/Madame_Bovary (accessed 291117)
3. https://en.wikipedia.org/wiki/Germinal_(novel) (accessed 291117)
4. https://en.wikipedia.org/wiki/The_Plague (accessed 291117)
5. https://en.wikipedia.org/wiki/Lord_of_the_Flies (accessed 301117)
6. https://en.wikipedia.org/wiki/1985_in_literature#Fiction (accessed 140120)
7. https://www.vox.com/culture/2017/3/2/14779892/barack-michelle-obama-65-million-book-deal-penguin-random-house (accessed 010520)

Robed

1. https://www.edeandravenscroft.com/ceremonial-dress/ (accessed 090620)
2. https://en.wikipedia.org/wiki/James_Mackay,_Baron_Mackay_of_Clashfern (accessed 090620)
3. Shakespeare, W. *Twelfth Night,* Act II, Scene V.

Collared

1. https://en.wikipedia.org/wiki/Biretta (accessed 291220)
2. https://en.wikipedia.org/wiki/Apethorpe_Hall (accessed 050520)
3. https://www.houseandgarden.co.uk/gallery/apethorpe-palace (accessed 100121)
4. https://en.wikipedia.org/wiki/Henry_Brassey,_1st_Baron_Brassey_of_Apethorpe (accessed 050520)
5. https://en.wikipedia.org/wiki/Richard_Ormston (accessed 291220)
6. https://www.lonepinehotel.com/ (accessed 291220)
7. Luke 1.31-32
8. https://en.wikipedia.org/wiki/Our_Lady_of_Walsingham (accessed 110620)
9. https://www.booking.com/hotel/es/rosarosae.en-gb.html (accessed 010121)
10. Michelin Tourist Guide Spain. 1995. Michelin et Cie. pp236-238
11. https://en.wikipedia.org/wiki/Botafumeiro#:~:text=The%20Botafumeiro%20(Galician%20for%20%27%22,swinging%20metal%20container%2C%20or%20censer. (accessed 130121)
12. Michelin Tourist Guide Spain. 1995. Michelin et Cie. p239
13. https://www.ermc.cam.ac.uk/ (accessed 291220)
14. https://en.wikipedia.org/wiki/Westminster_Abbey (accessed 270520)
15. http://www.dominicanlaity.ca/DominicanLaity/Events_files/LatinPronunciation.pdf (accessed 070520)
16. Matthew 20.26-27 (NEB)

Appendix A

1. Matthew 4.18-22
2. Ibid 10.2-4
3. Mark 3.16-19
4. Ibid 10,35-40
5. Ibid 5.21-24, 35-43; Luke 8.40-42, 49-56
6. Matthew 17.1-8; Mark 9.2-8; Luke 9.28-36
7. Matthew 26.36-46; Mark 14.32-42
8. John 21.17
9. Acts 1.13-14
10. Ibid 12.1-3
11. *The Penguin Dictionary of Saints.* 1965. Middlesex. Penguin Books Ltd. p182

***

Index

Notes

1. The author's novels are indexed; characters who feature in them are not.
2. The author is referred to as PRM throughout.
3. The fifth part, *Collared*, (pages 177-251) refers frequently to "Roman Catholicism", "Roman Catholic", "Anglo-Catholicism", "Church of England" "Holy Communion" and "Anglican" throughout. Those references are not indexed.
4. Dates of office-holding, when known, are stated, failing which "one-time" is used.
5. Appendices A and B are not indexed.

***